**A BOOK FROM/ABOUT/FOR THOSE WHO GO BEYOND THE TERRITORY OF THEIR DISCIPLINE.
EIGHT STORIES FROM BEYOND THE BORDERS**

Rat für Formgebung
German Design Council

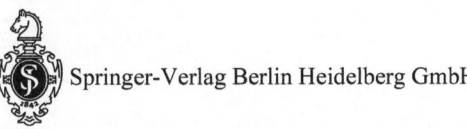
Springer-Verlag Berlin Heidelberg GmbH

ISBN 978-3-540-65589-3   ISBN 978-3-642-57037-7
DOI 10.1007/978-3-642-57037-7

Softcover reprint of the hardcover 1st edition 2002

T

HERE

YOU ARE

LOOKING

AT AND

TRAVELLING BEYOND

THIS EVER

CHANGING PLACE.

DIETER KRETSCHMANN
RAT FÜR FORMGEBUNG / GERMAN DESIGN COUNCIL

With the book series »Design im Kontext,« the Rat für Formgebung / German Design Council offers an international forum for art-related themes. The point is quite simply to provide stimulus, formulate new modes of thinking, and provoke discussion in all areas of art.

The world of visual communication has changed – not only in the fact that through the rapid development of digital technology, new possibilities for artistic expression are constantly emerging, but also in the fact that an increasing number of artists in all disciplines are using both old and new techniques that were not formerly seen as necessarily belonging to their respective disciplines.

Through this kind of overlap, or crossing of boundaries, results are being achieved which often arise from a close up of the various media, and which can no longer be placed into traditional categories.
The all-too-common pigeonholing of designer, artist, filmmaker, or illustrator needs to be re-thought – the rules are disintegrating, and we are being forced to abandon the systems which have thus far worked.

This eighth volume of the book series presents a small but significant selection of these developments and is itself a part of this new era of crossover within the intermedia artistic processes. Beyond the Borders is a forum for creative artists from diverse artistic disciplines who have, for the most part, conceived their contributions themselves and designed them especially for this book.

The idea for Beyond the Borders came out of the first profile intermedia conference in 1998, during which the theme »Crossover in Design, Art, Film and Music« was tackled in an international arena for the first time. Together with some of those who took part in this conference, and others who came later, members of Propellers have developed this »readable and watchable« book.

A book, which, through the contributions about P. Scott Makela and Tibor Kalman, both of whom, sadly, have recently passed away, has also become a homage to their thinking and oeuvre.

Mit der Schriftenreihe »Design im Kontext« bietet der Rat für Formgebung / German Design Council ein internationales Forum für Themen mit gestalterischem Bezug. Stets geht es darum, Anstöße zu geben, neue Denkansätze zu formulieren und Diskussionen in allen Bereichen der Gestaltung anzuregen.

Die visuelle Kommunikation hat sich verändert. Nicht nur, daß sich durch die rasante Entwicklung digitaler Techniken ständig neue gestalterische Möglichkeiten ergeben, sondern daß sich in zunehmendem Maße die Gestalter aller Professionen alter wie neuer Techniken bedienen, die bisher nicht unbedingt selbstverständlich für die jeweilige Disziplin waren.

Durch diese Grenzüberschreitungen werden Ergebnisse erzielt, die oftmals aus einer Verknüpfung der vielschichtigen Medien resultieren und kaum mehr eine klassische Einordnung zu lassen. Die Schubladen, in die man Designer, Künstler, Filmemacher oder Illustratoren nur allzu oft gesteckt hat, müssen neu kategorisiert werden, die Regeln lösen sich auf, man ist gezwungen, bisher gültige Systeme zu verlassen.

Der vorliegende achte Band der Schriftenreihe zeigt einen kleinen, prägnanten Ausschnitt dieser Entwicklungen und ist selbst ein Teil dieser neuen Ära der Crossover innerhalb intermediärer Gestaltungsprozesse. Beyond the Borders ist ein Forum für Kreative aus diversen gestalterischen Disziplinen, die zum Großteil ihren Beitrag selbst konzipiert und speziell für dieses Buch gestaltet haben.

Angeregt wurde Beyond the Borders durch die erste profile intermedia Konferenz im Jahr 1998, auf der sich internationale Referenten erstmals mit den »Crossover in Design, Kunst, Film und Musik« auseinandersetzten. Gemeinsam mit einigen der damals Beteiligten und neuen Akteuren entwickelten Mitglieder von Propellers dieses Bilder- und Lesebuch.

Ein Buch, das durch die Beiträge über P. Scott Makela und Tibor Kalman, die beide bedauerlicherweise vor kurzer Zeit verstorben sind, auch zu einer Hommage an ihre Gedanken und ihre Werke geworden ist.

DESIGN IS THINKING MADE VISUAL
SAUL BASS

TRAVELLING ON THE UNKNOWN PATH

THESE ARE EIGHT DIFFERENT STORIES (

FROM BEYOND EIGHT DIFFERENT BORDERS)

P. SCOTT & LAURIE HAYCOCK MAKELA
WITH PAUL SCHNEIDER/CRANBROOK

016 TO 041

Scott Makela and Laurie
Haycock Makela taught
together at Cranbrook
Academy of Arts in
Michigan. Both shared
a life between music
(their band: »audioafter-
birth«), graphic design
(their studio: »Words +
Images for Business +
Culture«), and teaching
(at Cranbrook).
Paul Schneider is a for-
mer student and now the
studio's senior designer.
(TRANSLATION ON PAGE 220)

YOU SHOCKED ME. THIS PIECE IS IN
MEMORY OF SCOTT, THE AFTERMATH
AND THE SUMMER OF HIS DEATH.
THE THREE SNOWBOARD PIECES WERE
HIS LAST WORK BEFORE HE DIED
FAR TOO EARLY ON MAY 7TH 1999.

Scott Makela und Laurie
Haycock Makela
unterrichteten gemeinsam
an der Cranbrook
Academy of Arts in Michi-
gan. Ihr gemeinsames
Leben bewegte sich
zwischen Musik (ihrer
Band: »Audioafterbirth«),
Grafik Design (ihrem
Studio: »Words + Images
for Business + Culture«)
und ihrer Lehrtätigkeit
(in Cranbrook).
Paul Schneider, ein ehe-
maliger Student, ist
heute der Senior-Designer
des Studios.
(ÜBERSETZUNG AUF SEITE 220)

YOU SHOCKED ME. DIESE ARBEIT
ENTSTAND IM GEDENKEN AN SCOTT,
AN DAS NACHBEBEN UND DEN
SOMMER SEINES TODES. DIE DREI
SNOWBOARD-ENTWÜRFE SIND SEINE
LETZTEN ARBEITEN BEVOR ER
AM 7. MAI 1999 VIEL ZU FRÜH STARB.

+ ACTION

IN MEMORY OF P. SCOTT MAKELA
BY LAURIE HAYCOCK MAKELA + PAUL SCHNEIDER

FAITH IN ACTION, GOD IS CLOSE, AND VERTIGO IS FUN
ARE THE LAST WORKS BY P. SCOTT MAKELA,
CREATED FOR ROSSIGNOL SKI AND SNOWBOARDS, APRIL 1999
VIDEO PHOTOGRAPHY BY DAVID CRABB, KURT MILLER, SEVRIN HENDERSON

ever onw
ard under
other skies

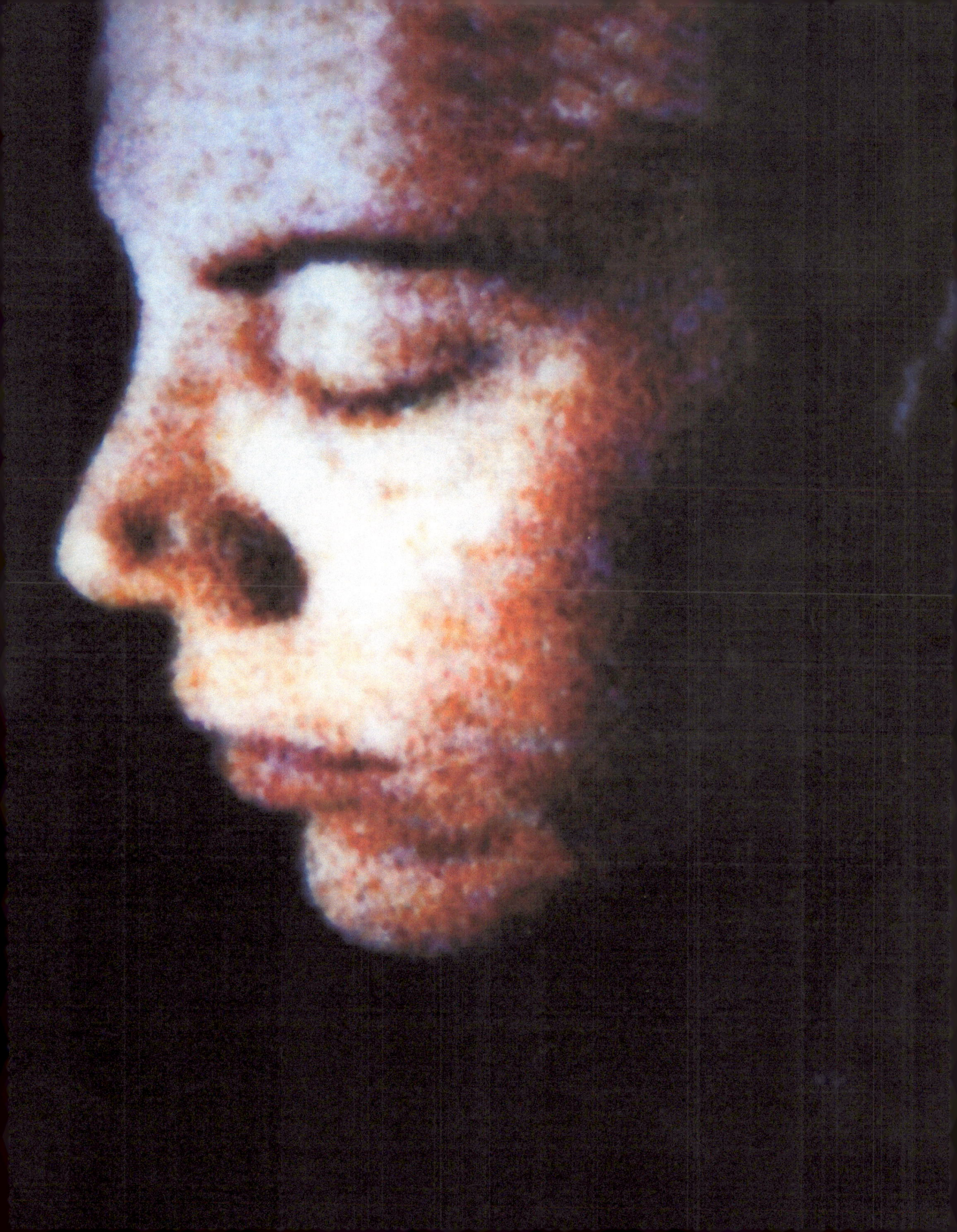

didja make that?

KEEPING SILENCE IS ONE OF
THE MOST POWERFUL PRACTICES IN
BUDDHISM. MOST OF YOUR TALK IS
SMALL CHATTER. WHEN YOU'RE
SILENT, YOU GET TO LISTEN.
FINDING FAULT WITH OTHER PEOPLE
CREATES LOTS OF SUFFERING.
IF YOU CAN REALLY NOT FIND FAULT
WITH ANYBODY AND ANYTHING,
YOU'LL BE AN EXTRAORDINARY
HAPPY PERSON.

IS

CLOSE

TO YF

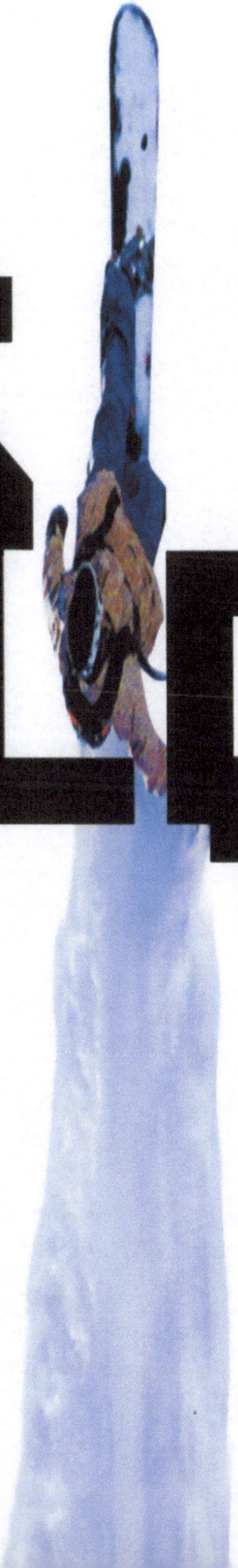

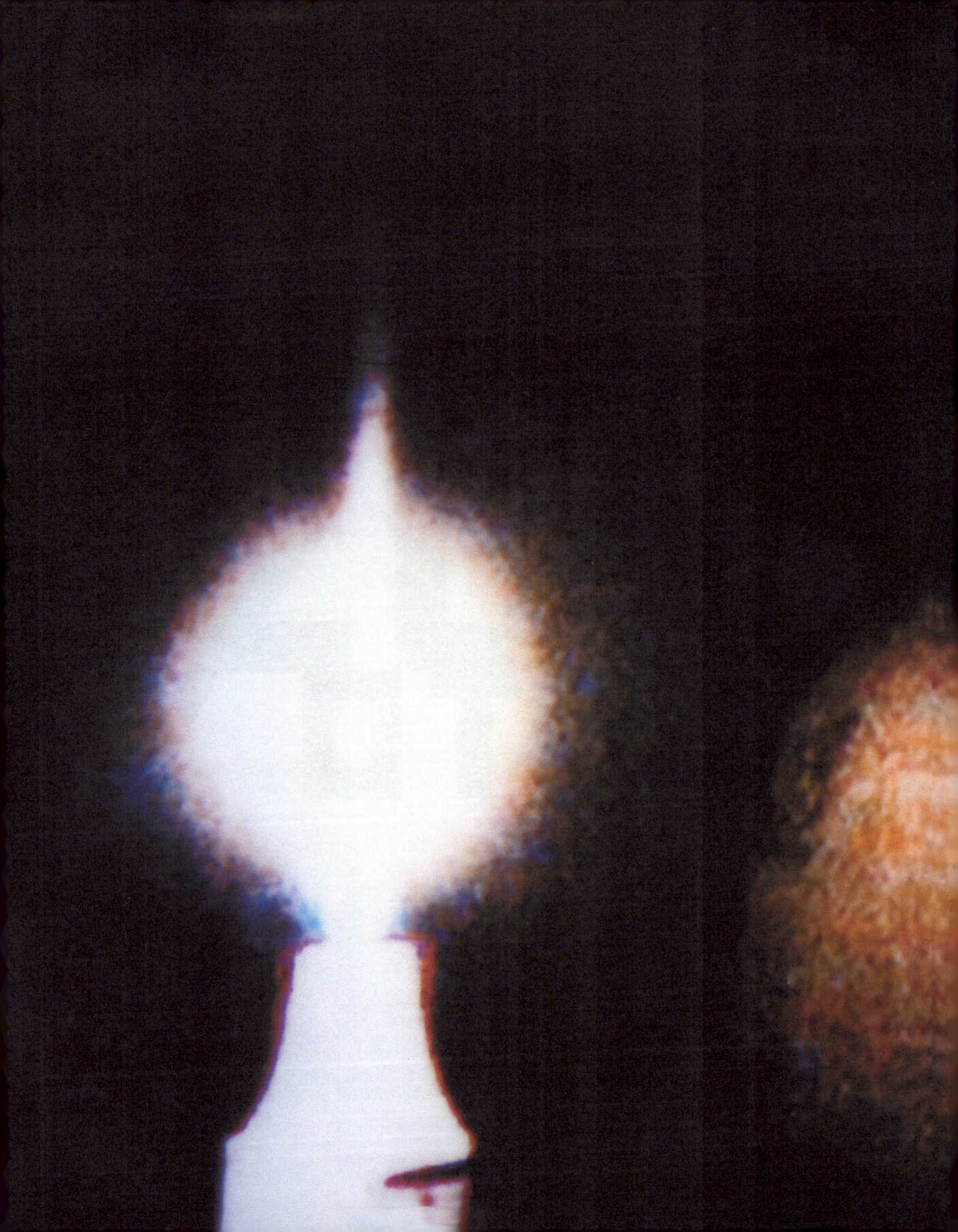

you shocked me.

did you hear that whip

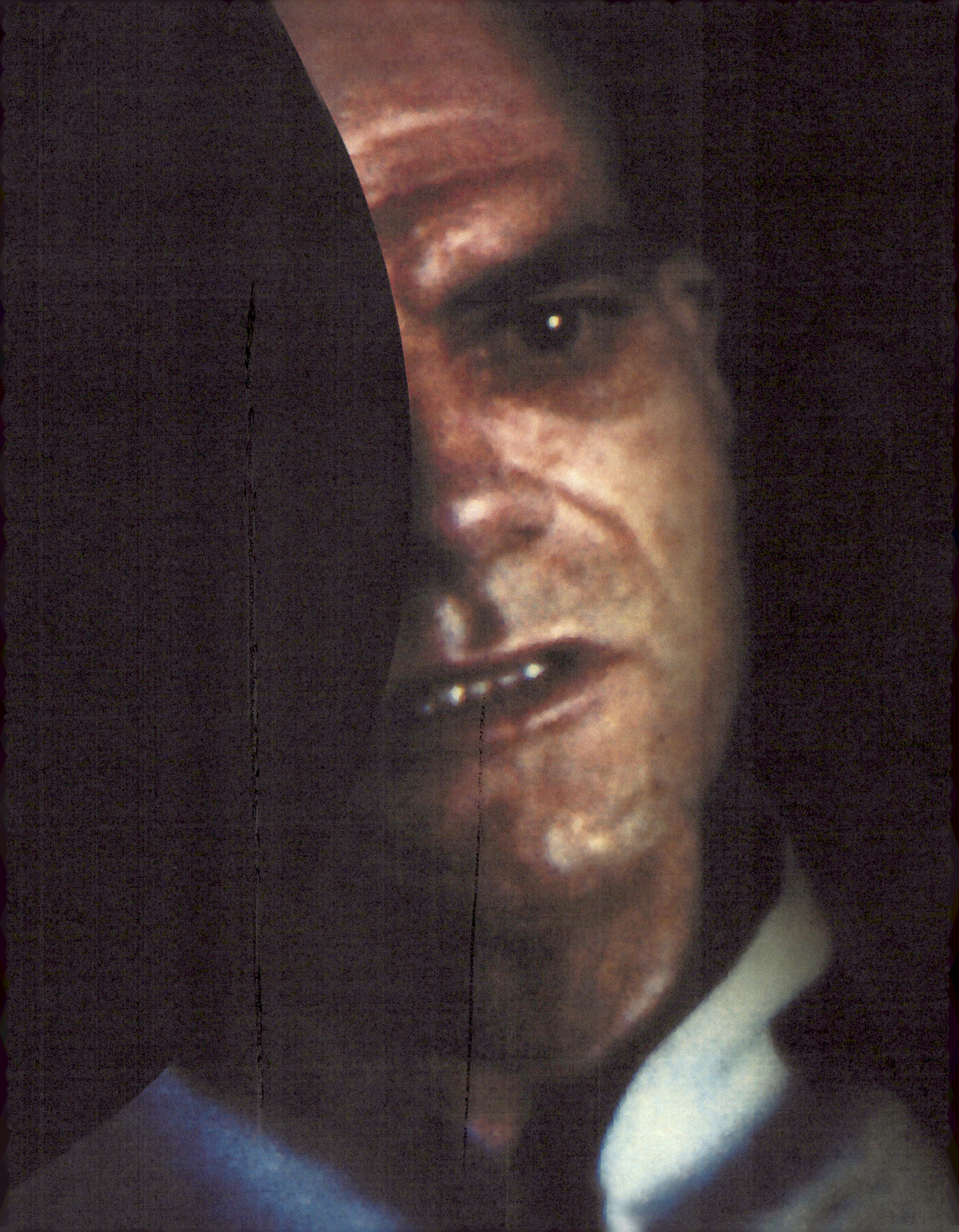

extreme
MEDITATION

THE SENSES ARE
TOOLS, NOT MASTERS.
THE BODY SAYS I'M
HUNGRY, I'M TIRED,
I NEED SEX, I WANT TO
WALK, BUT THE MIND CAN
PUT ALL OF THAT DOWN.
ON A 21-DAY RETREAT
WITH NO SLEEP, YOUR
MIND TELLS YOU IT'S
NOT POSSIBLE.
"TOGETHER-ACTION"
MAKES THIS POSSIBLE.
IN BUDDHISM WE SAY
"BY THE VIRTUE OF YOUR
HARD PRACTICE, I CAN DO
MY HARD PRACTICE."
EXTREME MEDITATION
PUTS YOU IN THE
HERE AND NOW.

GO
SFUN

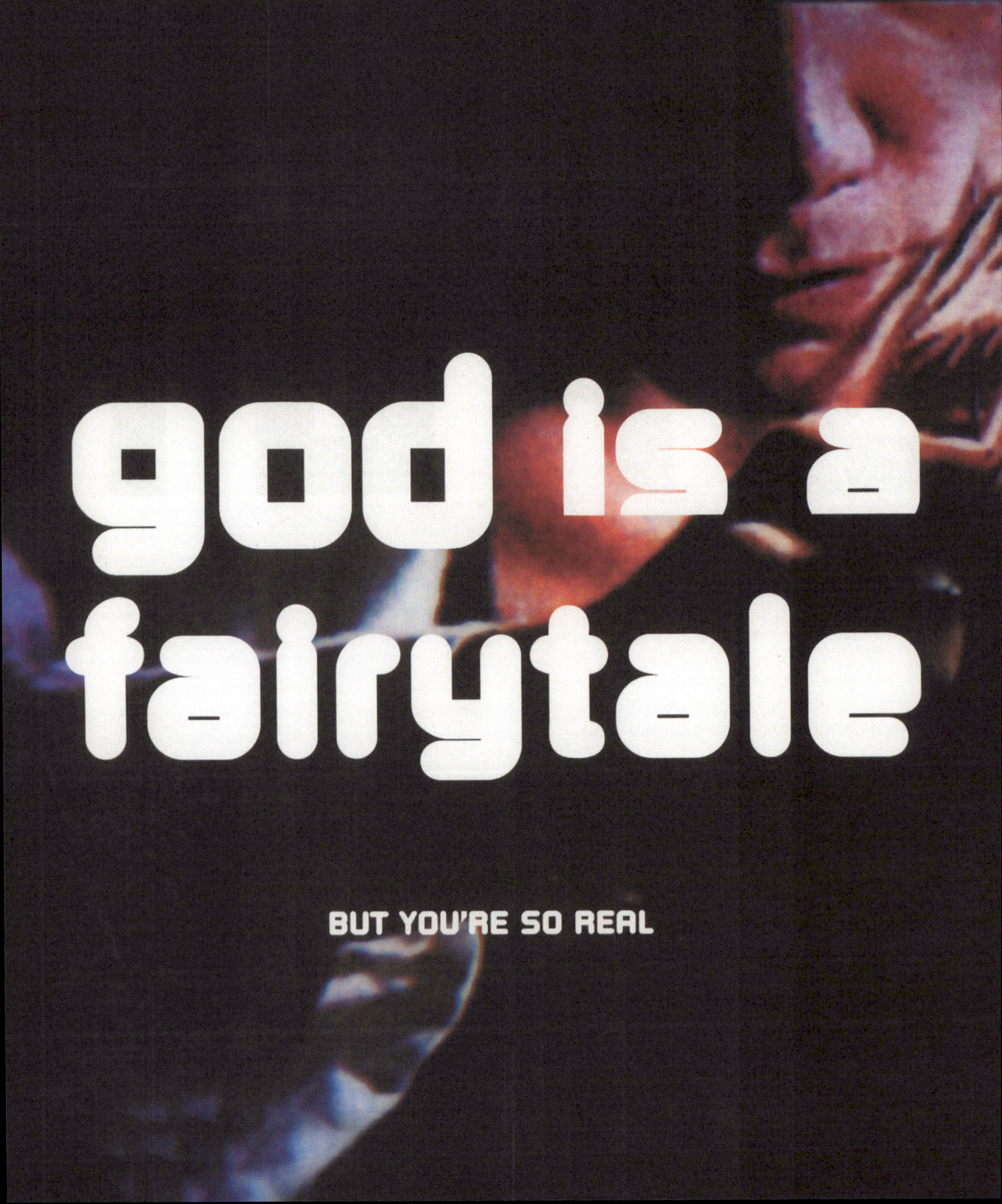
god is a fairytale
BUT YOU'RE SO REAL

did you see that?

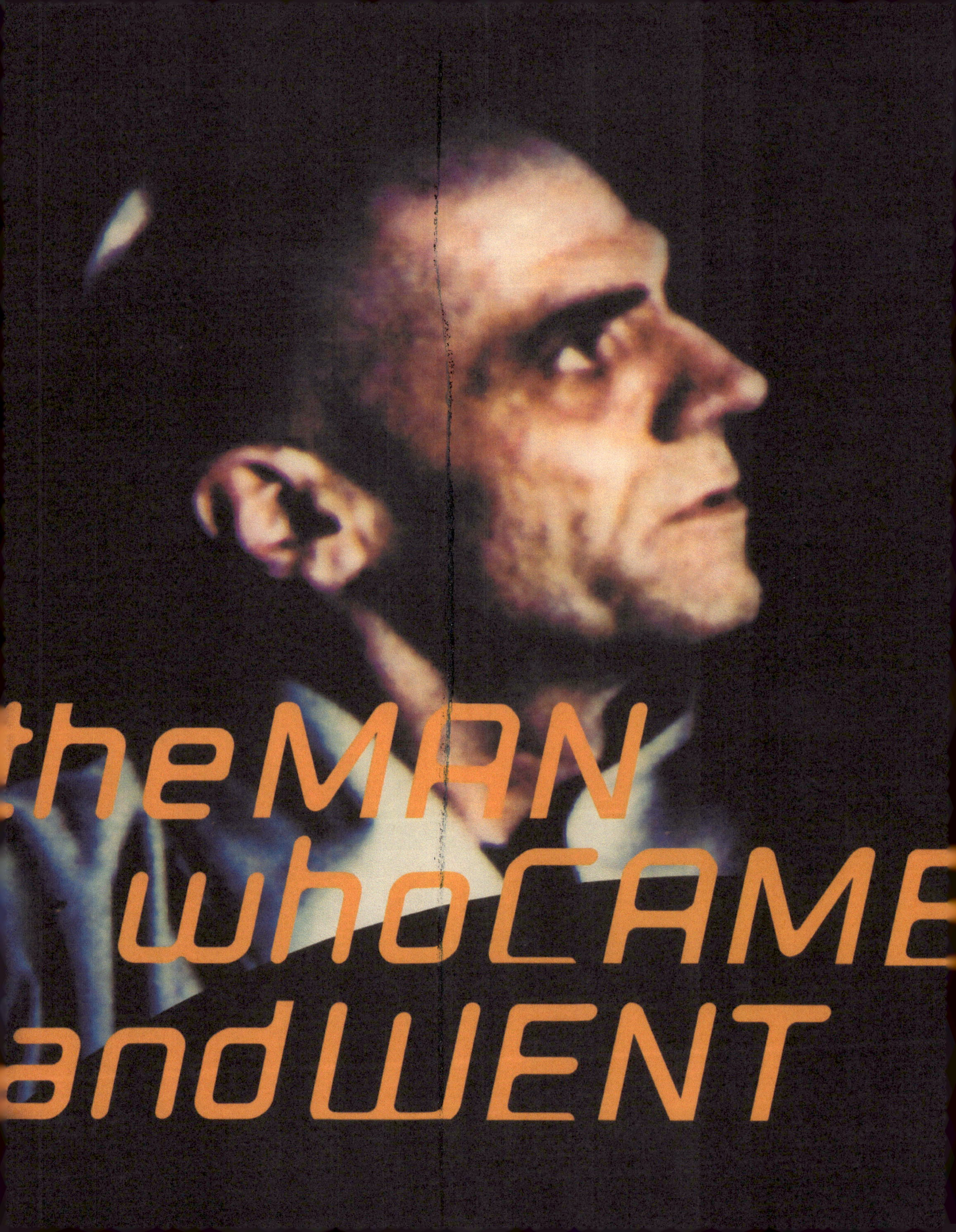

the MAN
whoCAME
andWENT

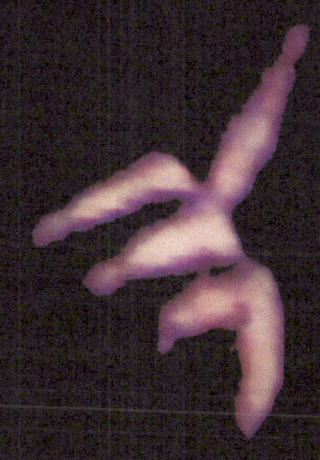

THROUGH ALL OF MY
CAUSE AND EFFECTS
I COME TO THIS WORLD
WITH THIS BODY. WHERE
WAS I BEFORE THIS BODY?
AND AFTER THIS BODY,
WHERE WILL I GO?
PEOPLE TREAT THEIR
"SELF" LIKE A POSSESSION.
BUT SELF IS JUST A
DREAM, BECAUSE WE
CHANGE. THE ESSENCE OF
MIND IS EMPTY. WHEN
YOU REALIZE THAT,
EVERYTHING BECOMES
FANTASTIC—A PROP,
A HOLOGRAM, A DREAM.
YOU CAN MOVE THROUGH
THESE LIVES WITHOUT
FEAR OF DEATH. YOU'RE
JUST ON A BUS WITH
PICTURES GOING BY.
HOW OLD ARE YOU? YOU'RE
AS OLD AS THE
BIG BANG. WASTE OF TIME
TO WORRY ABOUT PAST
LIVES.

PETER REA / LONDON

042 TO 069

As a »journeyman« of design he is a teacher in places with very different cultural backgrounds such as London, Philadelphia, Beirut, and Bremen. His home in Central London houses a vast »exhibition« of his life around the world and around design. But most of all he is the source of inspiration to countless projects like this book.

THIS PIECE IS THE UNFINISHED MAP OF PETER REA'S WAY TO SEE, EXPLAIN, AND DESIGN THE WORLD. HE IS A LIFELONG TEACHER AND INSPIRATOR FOR MANY GENERATIONS OF DESIGN STUDENTS.

Als ein »Journeyman« des Design, lehrt er an Orten mit sehr unterschiedlichen kulturellen Hintergründen wie London, Philadelphia, Beirut und Bremen. Seine Wohnung in Central London beherbergt eine grosse »Ausstellung« seines Lebens in den verschiedenen Ländern und aus der Welt des Designs. Doch vor allem ist er die Quelle der Inspiration für unzählige Projekte wie dieses Buch.

DIESE ARBEIT IST DIE UNVOLL-ENDETE (LAND)KARTE VON PETER REA'S ART, DIE WELT ZU SEHEN, SIE ZU ERKLÄREN UND SIE ZU ENTWERFEN. ER IST ZEITLEBENS LEHRER UND INSPIRATOR FÜR VIELE GENERATIONEN VON DESIGN-STUDENTEN.

lines of communication

the map of the world according to peter rea

I was bending down, pulling up my school socks again in the back street of Wimbledon as the first transatlantic jet plane, the comet, flew overhead. 1952. 'We live in the shadow of the ever accelerating pace of technology, what once took 500 years then took 300 then 30 now 3. People are continually waiting to invest in new ideas.' Buckminster Fuller, American visionary, said this at about the same time. ■ My virtual concept of the world then was formed by the smell of the waxed oilcloth map of the world which the geography master would tap. Tap, tap. And the pink pieces, these are the British Empire, nearly a third of the world. ■ My real concept was still limited by how far I could get and back on my roller skates or bike before it got dark. This measure of distance by hours of daylight still is a vital consideration. I discovered this from experience, walking out into the bush in Nigeria 25 years later. Watching the comet roar in the sky above London was a wonder equivalent to watching the concord flying today like a bird-plane, the only plane that looks as if it is meant to fly. Design in motion. ■ Until I was 8 or 9 my journeys were still dictated by playing marbles in the gutter. Eventually looking up to realise that home was out of sight.

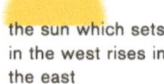

the sun which sets in the west rises in the east

Ich bückte mich in einer Seitenstraße in Wimbledon und zog meine Schulstrümpfe wieder hoch, als das erste transatlantische Düsenflugzeug, der Komet, über mir vorbeizog. 1952. »Wir leben im Schatten des sich immer schneller beschleunigenden Technologietempos. Was einst 500 Jahre gedauert hatte, dauerte später nur noch 300, dann 30 und jetzt 3 Jahre. Die Menschen warten ständig darauf, in neue Ideen zu investieren.« Buckminster Fuller, der amerikanische Visionär, sagte dies ungefähr zur gleichen Zeit. ▶ Mein virtuelles Weltkonzept wurde damals vom Duft der Wachstuch-Weltkarte geprägt, auf die der Geographielehrer mit seinem Stab klopfte. Klopf, klopf. Und die pink-farbenen Bereiche sind das Britische Imperium, fast ein Drittel der Welt. ▶ Mein reales Konzept war noch immer von der Tatsache bestimmt, wie weit weg ich mit meinen Rollschuhen oder dem Fahrrad fahren konnte und es dann wieder zurück schaffte, bevor es dunkel wurde. Dieses Messen von Entfernungen in Stunden des Tageslichts ist noch immer eine lebenswichtige Erwägung. Das habe ich aufgrund der Erfahrung, die ich machte als ich 25 Jahre später durch den nigerianischen Busch lief, festgestellt. ▶ Den Kometen am Himmel über London zu sehen glich einem Wunder, dem heute das Beobachten der Concorde gleichkommt, das Flugzeug, das noch immer wie ein Silbervogel fliegt – das einzige Flugzeug, das so aussieht, als sei es wirklich für das Fliegen bestimmt. Design in Bewegung. ▶ Bis zu meinem 8. oder 9. Lebensjahr waren meine Reisen noch vom Murmel-

NY 1984
photo: autotimer
or Ave Pildas, LA!
pr + jc

Amerikarma
exhibition invitation
ICA London 1973

44:45°

■ After the bike, when I was 16 came my first of 3 motorbikes. And the world started to open up into rolling countryside or the differences between East, West, North and South London. ■ My home has two world globes in it, on different floors of the house. A piece of string gives the concept of distance and journey times, as the crow flies, by wrapping the string around the world from point to point. When you look at the world from underneath, from Antarctica, then Russia to America is a much closer thing. Enough to see why one feared the other. The Soviet schoolmap places America not on our left but on their right, virtually connected to Canada by Alaska.

spielen am Straßenrand bestimmt. Irgendwann blickte ich auf und stellte fest, daß ich mein Zuhause nicht mehr sehen konnte. ▶ Dem Fahrrad folgte, sobald ich 16 war, mein erstes von drei Motorrädern. Und die Welt begann sich mir zu öffnen, in hügeligen Landschaften oder den Unterschieden zwischen Ost-, West-, Nord- und Süd-London. ▶ In meinem Zuhause stehen zwei Globen, in unterschiedlichen Stockwerken. Ein Stück Schnur bietet das schnellste Konzept für Entfernungen und Reisezeiten, ohne Umschweife, indem man die Schnur von einem Punkt zum andern Punkt auf die Weltkugel legt. ▶ Betrachtet man die Welt von unten her, von der Antarktis aus (mit der Schnur), dann liegen sich Rußland und Amerika wesentlich näher. Nahe genug, um zu erkennen, weshalb ein Land das andere fürchtete. Auf der sowjetischen Weltkarte in den Schulen liegt Amerika nicht links vom Betrachter sondern rechts. Die frühere Sowjetunion auf der linken Seite der Karte ist praktisch über Alaska mit Kanada verbunden.

my map of the world

My own map of the world is disjointed and reshaped by the basis of time not geography. It is in measurements of 4 to 5 hours of travel and an hour or two of preparation. ■ Across most of the world the nominal distance between centres of civilisation, farms, villages, settlements, cities is between 15 to 20 miles, 24 to 32 km. How far could be travelled in a day on foot or horseback before turning back, or going on, whilst the sun sets. ■ Halfway there, where? Turn back. Go on the same distance. My land-locked journeys on this island of ours take the same time as the children of the comet can fly me across the Atlantic or to Germany or the Middle East. Sometimes my traffic-locked struggles in and out and back across London take longer than my flights. My commuting is country to country.

■ My world is almost triangular in shape. The rest is out there, some-where. My lines of communication are not only telephone lines, railway lines, shipping lines, but airlines. ■ The sun rises in the east, sweeps an enormous arc in the sky to set in the west. Driving across America from New York to Los Angeles the sun seems always in front of you, setting over and over again. Travelling back to the east again the

Meine eigene Weltkarte ist auf der Basis der Zeit, nicht der Geographie, unterteilt und neu zusammengestellt. Im Maßstab von 4 bis 5 Stunden Reisezeit und einer bis zwei Stunden Vorbereitungszeit. ▶ In weiten Teilen der Welt liegt die nominale Entfernung zwischen Zivilisations-zentren, Farmen, Dörfern, Siedlungen oder Städten zwischen 15 und 20 Meilen, zwischen 24 und 32 Kilometern. Wie weit könnte man an einem Tag zu Fuß oder zu Pferd reisen, bevor man umkehren muß oder aber weitergeht, während die Sonne untergeht. Zur Hälfte dort – wo? ▶ Und kehrt Marsch. Oder geh die gleiche Entfernung weiter. Meine Reisen zu Lande auf dieser unserer Insel beanspruchen die gleiche Zeit, die die Nachkömmlinge des Kometen dazu benötigen, um mich über den Atlantik oder nach Deutschland oder in den Mittleren Osten zu befördern. Manchmal dauern meine verkehrs-bedingten Stauzeiten und der Kampf in und aus und durch London länger als meine Flüge.

Ich pendle von Land zu Land. Meine Welt hat eine fast dreieckige Form. Der Rest ist irgendwo da draußen. Meine Kommunikationslinien sind keine Telefonleitungen oder Bahnstrecken oder Schiffahrtswege, sondern Fluglinien. ▶ Kultur. Wenn ich am Nordpol meines Kompasses bin, dann wird die Kultur von meinem Südpol angezogen, wie Eisenspäne von einem Magnet. ▶ Die Sonne geht im Osten auf, schlägt einen riesigen Bogen am Himmel, um im Westen unterzugehen. Fährt man quer durch

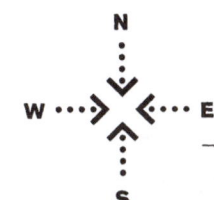

big western fireball in the sky warms your back and throws long shadows in front of you, over your shoulder. ■ Standing on my terrace in Lebanon I looked at the same sun setting in front of me into the Mediterranean. ■ Crossing the Peoples' Park of Bremen, Germany in the early morning of autumn, the leaves can be heard falling as the misty light cuts through the woods.

■ Looking at the blue scuddy clouds of Britain from below, or from above, the differences that were once so clearly marked on the school room map have been reformed into a new world of connections. Journeys are calculated by time not distance. ■ I am the north pole of my compass; culture is attracted to my south pole like iron filings to a magnet.

a person is not an island

Desert Island Disks is one of Britain's longest running radio programmes. Perhaps one day I will know if I am an island and what shape I am. Here are my 12 disks that I would take with me; and my book; and my luxury. And my wish (which isn't in the programme): to know what you would wish. My 12 disks are:

„Desert Island Disks" ist eine sehr bekannte Radiosendung in England. Vielleicht werde ich eines Tages erfahren, ob ich eine Insel bin und welche Form ich habe. Dies sind meine 12 Platten, die ich mitnehmen würde. Und mein Buch. Und mein Luxusobjekt. Und mein Wunsch: Ich würde gerne wissen, was Du Dir wünschen würdest. Meine 12 Platten sind:

Ain't misbehavin: played by Fats Waller

Old rocking chair: Humphrey Lytellton

Misty: Errol Garner

Midnight hour blues: Leroy Carr and Scrapper Blackwell

Black magic woman: Santana

Dark side of the moon: Pink Floyd

Mood indigo: Duke Ellington and Johnny Hodges

Bird on a wire: Joe Cocker

Brown sugar: Rolling Stones

Dubnoheadwithyourbassman: underworld

House for sale: Chuck Berry

Blue skies smiling at you: Irving Berlin

Flying home: Lionel Hampton

The times they are a changing: Bob Dylan

Yara, and Maarifti Feek: Fairouz

Fool on the hill: Beatles

The photographer: Philip Glass

Basin Street Blues: Louis Armstrong and the All Stars

Rock around the olock: Bill Haley and the comets

Steamboat stomp: King Oliver

Shall we swing a little: George Shearing and Peggy Lee

Sunny side of the street: Ella and Basie

The 1938 carnegie hall concert: Benny Goodman

Entry to New York: Joe Zawinul

Monk's blues: Thelonious Monk

Concerto for viola in E: because men can cry too

Konzert für Viola in E: Weil Menschen weinen können

The book: Cannery Row and Of Mice and Men: John Steinbeck

Luxury: Cooking pots (and my memory)

Luxusobjekt: Kochtöpfe (und meine Gedächtnis)

Amerika, von New York nach Los Angeles, so steht die Sonne immer vor dir. Auf der Rückreise in den Osten wärmt der große, westliche Feuerball deinen Rücken und wirft lange Schatten vor dich, über deine Schulter. Stehe ich auf meiner Terrasse im Libanon, sehe ich dieselbe Sonne vor mir im Mittelmeer untergehen. Durchquert man den Volkspark in Bremen an einem frühen Herbstmorgen, kann man die Blätter fallen hören, während das neblige Licht durch die Bäume fällt. Schaut man die Wolken und den Himmel

über Großbritannien von unten oder von oben an, erkennt man, daß die einst auf der Klassenzimmer-Weltkarte so deutlich gekennzeichneten Unterschiede zu einer neuen Welt von Verbindungen umgeformt wurden. ▸ Reisen werden anhand von Zeit, nicht anhand von Entfernungen, berechnet. ▸ Wenn ich der Nordpol an meinem Kompass bin, dann wird die Kultur von meinem Südpol angezogen wie Eisenspäne von einem Magneten.

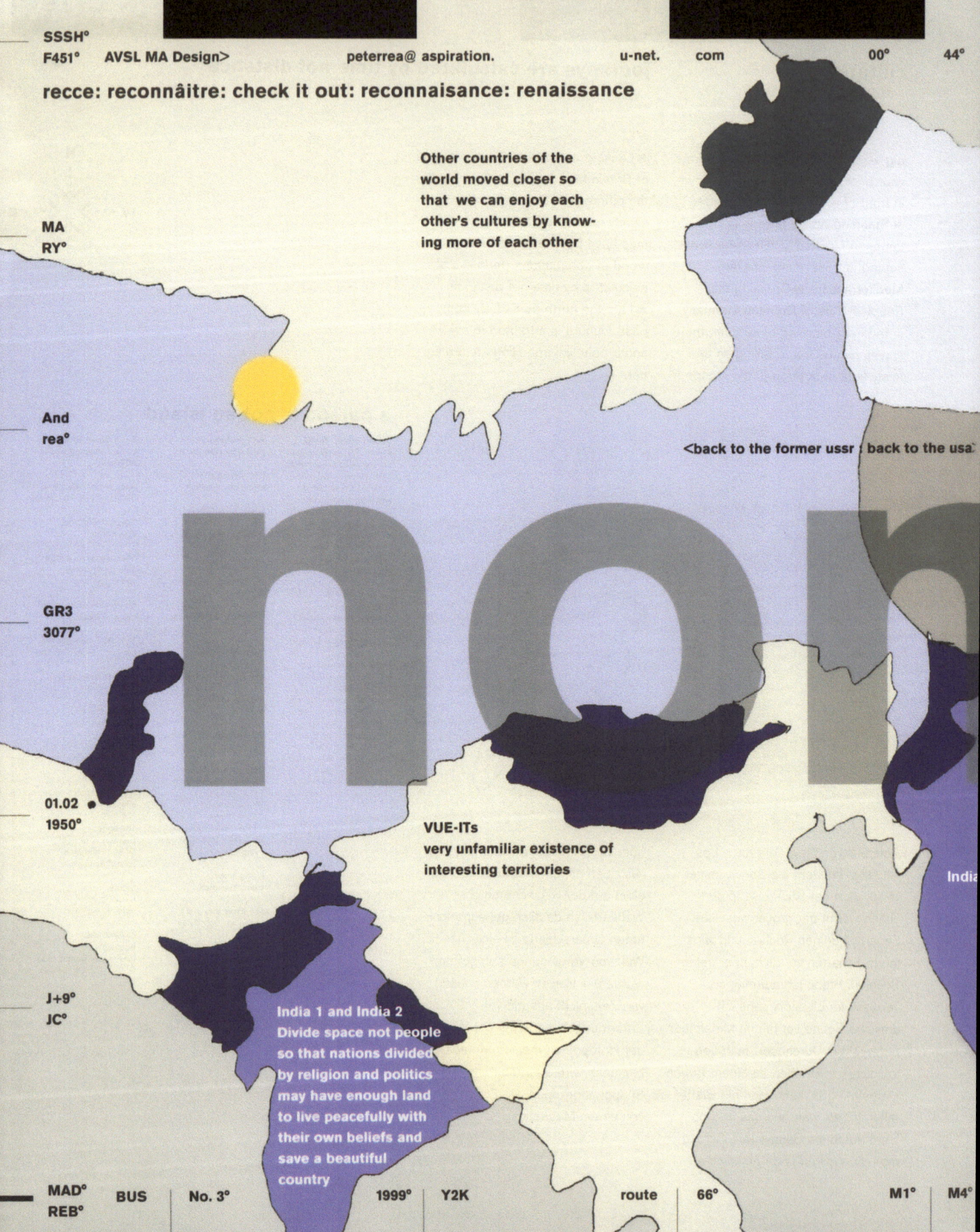

Other countries of the
world moved closer so
that we can enjoy each
other's cultures by know-
ing more of each other

MA
RY°

And
rea°

<back to the former ussr : back to the usa>

GR3
3077°

01.02 ●
1950°

VUE-ITs
very unfamiliar existence of
interesting territories

India

J+9°
JC°

India 1 and India 2
Divide space not people
so that nations divided
by religion and politics
may have enough land
to live peacefully with
their own beliefs and
save a beautiful
country

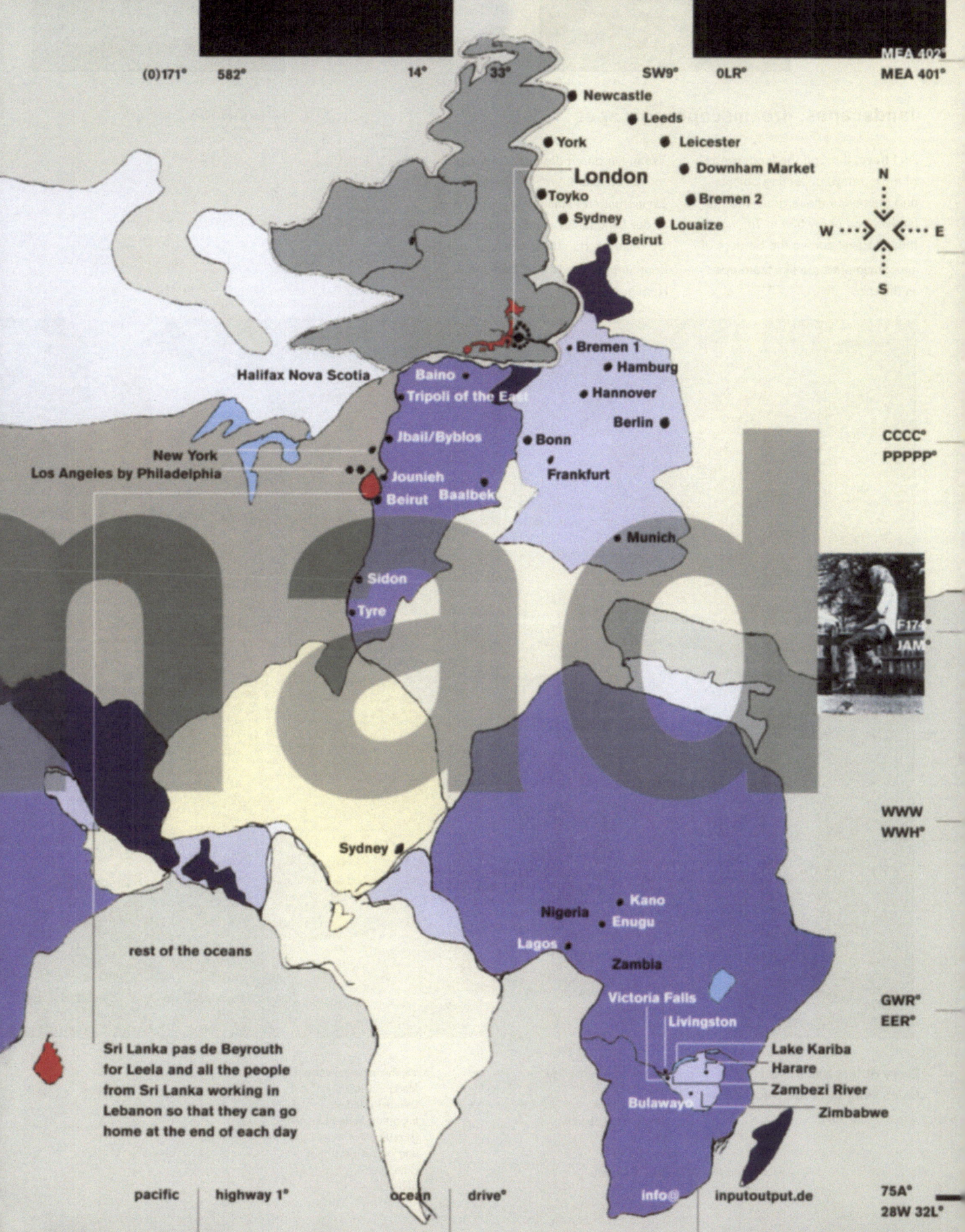

landscapes, dreamscapes, escapes

Now this is what I call a »living« room

As I travel through the landscapes of my journeys collecting objects and memories these grow into the landscapes of my home. Through these I travel across the borders of time: memories are like teardrops in the rain.

Wenn ich durch die Landschaften meiner Reisen fahre, Dinge und Erinnerungen sammele wachsen diese in der Landschaft meines Hauses. So reise ich durch die Grenzen der Zeit. Erinnnerungen sind wie Tränen im Regen.

Every object has a story
Jedes Ding hat eine Geschichte

From his master's voice
Made in Britain
Played in India
Imported to Lebanon
bought
brought
back to Britain

Von his masters voice
Made in Britain
Benutzt in Indien
Importiert in den Libanon
gekauft
und wieder nach
Britannien
gebracht

f.22

Wie weit ist zu weit
wenn Du unendlich
weit schauen
kannst. Wahr-
nehmung kommt
mit dem Alter.
Das ist ein gutes
Alter: Y2K

how far is too far if
you can see to infinity;
perception comes
with age, this is a
good age: Y2K

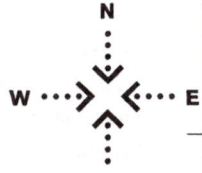

>
ARD 4000 hi fi
Made in Britain
product design by
pr
ARD 2000 series
designed 1967
ARD 4000 1974

>
ARD 4000 HiFi
Made in Britain
Produktdesign von
pr
ARD 2000 Serie
Design 1967
ARD 4000 1974

Skyscape:
Basil Town
artist and
teacher

Skyscape:
Basil Town
Künstler
und Lehrer

Apples are not the only fruit

Äpfel sind nicht die einzigen Früchte

Landscape 1999
photo: pr with Stuart Brown

why do I wear two shirts?

I am interested in the layers of meaning, layers of clothes. Why do I carry two of everything in the boot of my Mustang? Track shoes and Lumberjack boots. Two shirts. Waistcoats. Couple of afghan coats of sheepskin. ■ I was first asked this question in America. Philadelphia 1971. And in Philadelphia at that time of year I had two pairs of jeans on. It was cold and I mean cold. But not as cold as 20 years later in Halifax Nova Scotia Canada. There the breath froze my eyebrows stiff and the car of that time just froze all over in a snow white-out at 100 km per hour, 65 mph reduced down to zero speed and temperature in as many seconds. An igloo on wheels. No vision. Immovable in a country of boats frozen to the land. Sea frozen into sculptured waves. Stuck. ■ Well I am curious to know what is going to happen. What lies below the surface, underneath. I like the exploration and revelation of the unknown. Be prepared like Lara the Tomb Raider, always have something in my pack. Battle fatigue one minute, deep sea swimming the next. Bathing in the sun and under the moon. Like the night in San Juan below LA on the Mexican border, under the moonlight sitting in a hot jacussi on a porch watching the stars with martinis. ■ Why do I wear two shirts? My fascination is in the balance of power between form or function, form and function. The opposition of this to that, 'well it can be like this or could be like that!', young to old, wisdom and whizz, smooth and the rough. Rough on the smooth. Tactile.

layers of meaning

Sensations are my second skin. For the past 30 years I have been working in more than one country. Uncovering different cultures. This is as interesting as covering and uncovering the human body. Seeing one layer next to another, adding one culture to another and without losing either.

Ich interessiere mich für Bedeutungsschichten, Kleidungsschichten. ▶ Weshalb habe ich von allem zwei Ausgaben im Kofferraum meines Mustangs? Diese Frage wurde mir zum ersten Mal in Amerika gestellt. Philadelphia 1971. Laufschuhe und Wanderschuhe. Zwei Hemden. Jacken. Ein Paar afghanische Schafwollmäntel. Und in Philadelphia um diese Jahreszeit zwei Paar Jeans an. Es war kalt – und ich meine: richtig kalt. Aber nicht so kalt, wie 20 Jahre später in Halifax, Neuschottland, Kanada. (Dort froren mir die Augenbrauen vom Atem steif und mein damaliges Auto fror komplett bei einem Schneesturm ein, bei 100 km/h, die in null Komma nichts auf Nulltempo und -temperatur fielen. Ein Iglu auf Rädern. Keine Sicht. Unbeweglich. Ein Land voller Boote, die ans Land gefroren waren. Das Meer in plastischen Wellen gefroren. Stillstand.) ▶ Die Neugier will mich wissen lassen, was unter der Oberfläche ist, darunter. Ich mag die Erkundung und Offenbarungen des Unbekannten. Sei bereit wie Lara, die Tomb Raider-Figur, habe immer etwas parat im Rucksack. Kampfesmüdigkeit in einem Moment, Tiefseeschwimmen im nächsten. Ein Bad unter der Sonne und dem Mond. Wie in der Nacht in San Juan, südlich von Los Angeles an der mexikanischen Grenze, im Mondlicht in einem heißen Whirlpool auf einer Veranda, die Sterne mit Martinis betrachtend. ▶ Weshalb trage ich zwei Hemden? Meine Faszination ist das Gleichgewicht der Kräfte zwischen Form und Funktion. Die Opposition zwischen diesem und jenem, »Nun, es kann so oder könnte anders sein!«, jung und alt, Weisheit und Witz, glattem und rauhem. Das rauhe und das glatte. Taktil. Empfindungen sind meine zweite Haut. ▶ In den letzten 30 Jahren habe ich in mehr als einem Land gearbeitet. Unterschiedliche Kulturen entdeckt. Das ist so interessant wie das Zudecken oder Aufdecken des menschlichen Körpers. Eine Schicht neben der anderen sehen, und eine Kultur einer anderen hinzufügend, ohne eine davon zu verlieren.

Geschichtenerzählen:
alles hat eine Geschichte
Reisen der Neugier

Erinnerungen an das nie Gekannte
Ich bin der Nordwind,
der über fremde Formen weht.
Ich kräusle mich dicht über dem Boden
und folge den Windungen des Landes.
Mein Atem ist wie eine zweite Haut.
Ich bin.
Der warme, brennend heiße Wind der
Sahara, der sich in die Täler legt,
über die Ebenen strömt,
mit dem Bergrücken kollidiert.
Einen feinen Staubfilm hinterläßt,
der in ferne Länder entschwindet.
Sich in Poren und Rissen ansammelt,
in tiefen und höhlenhaften,
mysteriösen Öffnungen versickert.
Ich bin der Anfang
des Regens. Ich falle hier und da.
Und dort, und dort, und da.
Ich bin der Wasserfall der über die
Felsen gleitet,
Der schmettert und kracht und
In dem tiefen, purpurfarbenen Teich zur
Ruhe kommt bevor er zum Meer eilt.
Ich bin diese Oase,
die zwischen Bergen und dem Meer in
einem Tal liegt.
Die aus Milch und Honig besteht und die
Sonne
endlos
auf- und untergehen sieht.
Ich bin der Mond am Tag,
blaß, doch immer da.
Ich bin der Wind, der warme Ostwind,
der der Sonne
in den Westen nacheilt.

Training ground:
Als der Zug abfuhr,
hatte ich das Gefühl, in einem Film von
Peter Greenaway, Ridley Scott,
Derek Jarman oder Lara Saba zu leben.
Ein Echo zertrümmerte meine
Melancholie und Erinnerungen begannen
schon zu entstehen, um wie Tränen im
Regen zu fallen.

Story telling:
everything has a story
Journeys of curiosity

Memories of the never known:
I am the north wind
which blows across foreign forms,
I curl close to the ground and follow
the curves of the land.
my breath is like a second skin.
I am.
the warm searing hot wind of the Sahara
settling in the valleys, streaming
across the plains,
colliding with the mountain range.
leaving a fine film of dust
which vanishes in foreign lands.
collecting in the pores and cracks,
disappearing
into deep and cavernous, mysterious
holes.
I am the beginning
of rain. I drop here and there.
And there, and there, and there.
I am the waterfall which slides over
the boulders,
which smashes and crashes down
to rest
in the deep, purple pool before rushing
to the sea.
I am that oasis
which lies between
mountain and ocean in a valley
of milk and honey which sees the sun
rise and set
interminably.
I am that moon in the day,
pale but always there.
I am the wind, the warm wind of the east
which follows the sun
to the west.

Training ground:
as the train pulled out
I felt I was living in a movie
by peter greenaway, ridley scott,
wim wenders, derek jarman
or lara saba.
an echo shattered my melancholy
and memories were already forming
to drop
like tears in the rain.

photographs:
by Janine Wiedel 1973

intermedia

beware: heavy duty equipment at the junction

'Now we have landed where the hand of man never set foot'–James Joyce. ■ Intermedia is as simple as it sounds and can be as complex as it looks. It is an activity where people interested in moving out of their territorial limits may do so. It is the crossover: the junction between art, design, music, performance, photography, video and film. Each technological change has given a push and a shove to move on, or change direction. As a colleague once said: technology is like a steam roller; you either stand in the way and try to stop it (with results which may flatten more than an ego) or get in the driving seat. Intermedia is a meeting point at the crossroads of creativity. A meeting point which previously was less accessible. ■ Working in theatre for more than a year led me to combine my graphic interests with those of psychedelic happenings in the sixties. Building theatrical environments with slide projection and film projection onto walls and ceilings.

Using smoke, and thunder flashes, making unbearable contrasts of noise and image. Music and sound. Freeform Son et Lumiere. ■ Strapping banks of Kodak carousel projectors together, playing the resulting keyboard of hand controls like an image organ, made images rush across the screen. Stacking the projectors in all sorts of configurations, let images climb up the wall, drop down and move in any or all directions at once. Reflected through mirrors. Seen through multiple layers of semi-transparent screens. Destroying the frame, involving the viewer in the environment. ■ The keyboard of controls connected image to music to rhythm to soundtrack. And stripping in black areas by blanking out the light-fall within the overall projection areas, using masks, would allow me to insert smaller fields of moving image from Super-8 and 35 mm film projectors. ■ I learned that to work with a team of people gave more achievement, not less work. And that all my journeys into this mixed media were always going to mean more, much more

work. ■ This shift from flat graphics, typographics into three dimensions, sound, light and moving-image wasn't a replacement for anything but an addition. ■ Single specialisations can lead to quality and depth. Like digging a very deep hole into a subject. Sometimes this is so deep and of such a narrow diameter that many people walk on by. Not noticing anything except the hole, trying to avoid it. Unaware that anyone is down it. For myself I feel I have sacrificed that which comes with one recognisable specialisation but have moved side to side crossing boundaries. Looking out from the window of the train or plane. Stopping the car on the motorway, turning off down a side road. Wasting time talking, walking, thinking around the question. ■ Sociological studies show that the two minorities in the take-up of new ideas are the pioneers and the traditionalists. In the middle sit the rest in three main groups: the Early Adopters, the Late Adopters (the largest

▶ »Now we have landed where the hand of man never set foot« – James Joyce Intermedia ist so einfach wie es klingt und kann so komplex sein, wie es aussieht. Es ist eine Aktivität, bei der Menschen, die daran interessiert sind, ihre Grenzen zu übertreten, dies auch tun können. Es ist die Verbindung von Kunst, Design, Musik, Performance, Fotografie, Video und Film. Jede technologische Veränderung hat den Anstoß zur Fortbewegung oder Veränderung gegeben. Wie ein Kollege einmal sagte: Technologie ist wie eine Dampfwalze, man steht ihr entweder im Weg und versucht sie anzuhalten (mit Konsequenzen, die mehr als nur ein Ego plattdrücken), oder man sitzt in ihrem Führersitz. ▶ Über ein Jahr lang habe ich am Theater gearbeitet, als ich eigentlich mein Design ausbauen sollte, und der

Umstand, nicht in einen TV-Regisseurkurs aufgenommen worden zu sein, führten mich dazu, in den 60er Jahren meine grafischen Interessen mit psychedelischen Happenings zu kombinieren. Ich baute theatralische Umgebungen mit Dia- und Filmprojektionen auf Wände und Decken. Verwendete Rauch und Donnerblitze, inszenierte unerträgliche Kontraste aus Lärm und Bildern. Musik und Ton. Son et Lumiere. ▶ Ich verband Reihen von Diaprojektoren miteinander, spielte auf den Fernbedienungen wie auf einer Bildorgel und jagte Bilder über die Leinwand. Ich stapelte die Projektoren in allen möglichen Konfigurationen, ließ Bilder die Wand hochklettern, hinunterfallen und gleichzeitig in jede oder alle Richtungen wandern. Reflektierte sie mit Spiegeln. Den Rahmen zerstörend, den Betrachter

in die Umgebung integrierend.
▶ Ich lernte, daß die Arbeit mit einem Team zu mehr Leistung, nicht zu weniger Arbeit, führte. Und daß all meine Reisen in dieses gemischte Medium immer mehr, viel mehr Arbeit bedeuten würden. ▶ Diese Bewegung weg von flachen Grafiken, prinzipiell Typografien in drei Dimensionen, Ton, Licht und bewegten Bildern, war kein Ersatz für irgendetwas, sondern eine Ergänzung. ▶ Spezialisierungen können zu Qualität und Tiefe führen. Als ob man ein sehr tiefes Loch in ein Thema gräbt. Manchmal ist es so tief und so eng, daß viele Menschen daran vorübergehen. Nichts wahrnehmend außer dem Loch und dem Versuch, es zu meiden. Was mich betrifft, meine ich, daß ich das, was mit einer erkennbaren Spezialisierung einhergeht, geopfert habe und mich stattdessen von

technological change
des pr/photos jc 1991
digital images:
Carlo Tartaglia

the hand of man: announcement for profile intermedia 1:
the international conference on the crossover in media
Bremen 1998: des: the profile 1 team

group) and the Reactionaries (an equally large group). Traditionalists hold on to standards and principles like the tail to a kite, keeping stable in a stormy sky. But today's kites have no tail and use two hands and a lot of physical effort to control them. And new technologies seem to be like wild horses which have to get mounted to get the best from them. Especially if you want to go where only wild horses can take you. ■ These shifts in possibilities, for people like graphic designers who have otherwise been tied firmly to two dimensions and static speechless images, makes breaking the rules all the more interesting. The image exists not in a frame but in a free relationship with the context, its environment. Intermedia people seem to become ideas' factories. ■ The evolution of the electronic synthesiser in music is an ideal metaphor for the development of intermedia or the new technology as creative instruments. The synthesiser appeared in the small ensemble, or in the string quartet or in the jazz or pop world as a substitute for a piano, violin or saxophone: crossing all boundaries as first an imitator and then as an individual new creative instrument. Like the synthesiser the computer it is not just a tool as many would have it. ■ With digital electronics the perception of music has been revolutionised. John Cage's and Stockhausen's day of graphic compositions which were still fixed to the page, even though they achieved indeterminate music, have become unfixed composition and performances buried deep in the memory banks of digital configurations. When released these digits become music to our eyes and images to our ears. ■ The history and the parts of intermedia are not necessarily anything to do with computers although that is the technology which has turned push into pull. We are somewhere in a new territory where the hand of man has never set foot.

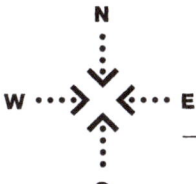

l. moholy-nagy

einer Seite zur anderen bewegt habe, und dabei Grenzen überschritten habe.
▶ Soziologische Studien zeigen, daß die beiden Minderheiten, die eine neue Idee aufnehmen, die Pioniere und die Traditionalisten sind. Dazwischen sitzt der Rest, in drei Gruppen unterteilt: die frühen Annehmer, die späten Annehmer (die größte Gruppe) und die Reaktionäre (eine ebenfalls große Gruppe). Die Traditionalisten halten an Maßstäben und Prinzipien fest wie der Schwanz an einem Drachen, der ihn am stürmischen Himmel hält. Doch die heutigen Drachen haben keinen Schwanz mehr, und man braucht beide Hände und einen hohen körperlichen Einsatz, um sie zu kontrollieren. Und neue Technologien scheinen wie wilde Pferde, die beritten werden müssen, um das beste aus ihnen herauszuholen. Vor allem, wenn du dort hin willst, wohin nur wilde Pferde dich bringen können. ▶ Diese Veränderung der Möglichkeiten, zum Beispiel für Grafikdesigner, die bisher fest an zwei Dimensionen und statische, wortlose Bilder gebunden waren, macht das Brechen der Regeln um so interessanter. ▶ Die Entwicklung des elektronischen Synthesizers in der Musik ist eine ideale Metapher für die Entwicklung von Intermedia oder der neuen Technologie als kreatives Instrument. Der Synthesizer trat im kleinen Ensemble, im Streichquartett oder der Jazz- bzw. Popwelt als Ersatz für ein Piano, eine Violine oder ein Saxophon auf: Er überschritt alle Grenzen, zuerst als Imitator, und dann Signifikant als individuelles, neues, kreatives Instrument. Wie der Synthesizer ist auch der Computer nicht nur ein Werkzeug, auch wenn das vielen am liebsten wäre. ▶ Musik wurde durch Elektronik revolutioniert. Aus John Cages und Stockhausens Zeit der grafischen Kompositionen, die – auch wenn sie eine unbestimmte Musik erzeugten – noch an das Stück Papier gebunden waren, entwickelten sich ungebundene Kompositionen und Performances, die tief in den Memory-Datenbanken digitaler Konfigurationen vergraben sind. Wenn sie freigesetzt werden, werden diese Zahlen zu Musik für unsere Augen und zu Bildern für unsere Ohren. ▶ Die Geschichte und die Teile der Gesamtheit von Intermedia hat nicht zwingend etwas mit Computern zu tun, auch wenn dies die Technologie ist, die als Zugpferd dient. Wir befinden uns irgendwo in einem neuen Territorium »where the hand of man has never set foot.«

pr as atlas
photo: Janine Wiedel 1984

from Tripoli looking east
photo: pr 1998

moholy nagy:
intermedia pioneer
catalogue and exhibition
by pr 1980

useful visas

nützliche Visas

für schwieriges
Gelände

life isn't a rehearsal

Das Leben ist
keine Übung

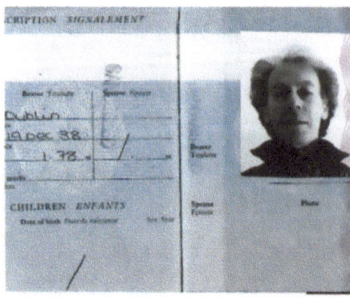

it's not (just) what
you do, it's the way
that you do it

Es kommt nicht (nur) darauf an,
was man tut,
es kommt darauf an,
wie man es tut

wisdom and
whizz kids
work together

wisdom und
whizz kids
arbeiten
zusammen

as you shout into
the wood so you
will hear the echo

Wie man in den
Wald hineinruft,
so schallt es
zurück

never get on
a pedestal

Erhebe Dich
nie auf
ein Podest

tea break

Teepause

music is my
mistress,
duke ellington

Die Musik ist
meine Mätresse,
Duke Ellington

education and
design are my
mistresses

Bildung und
Design sind
meine
Mätressen

They can because
they think they can,
Virgil

Sie können,
weil Sie glauben, daß sie es können,
Virgil

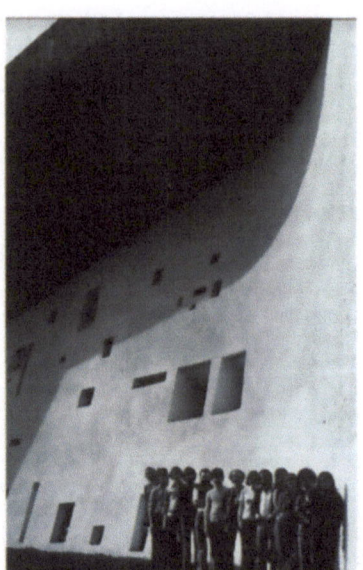

other people have
problems too:
GOD flat on his
back: 'I could
use a few "Praise
Hims" just now'

Andere haben
auch Probleme:
GOTT, auf dem
Rücken liegend:
„Ich könnte jetzt
ein paar
Lobpreisungen
vertragen"

s/he knows
s/he will because
s/he knows s/he can

Sie/er weiß,
daß Sie/Er es tun wird,
weil Sie/Er weiß, daß Sie/Er es kann.

act don't react

Agieren nicht
reagieren

snooze you lose

Wer schläft
verliert

who can know
what the future
can hold?

Wer weiß,
was die Zukunft
bringt?

see with your ears
hear with your eyes

Schau mit den
Ohren
Höre mit den
Augen

New Intermedia Center
Offenes Atelier 1997

Freitag, 7. 2. bis Sonntag, 9. 2.
10 bis 20 Uhr
Raum 126, 1. Stock
Dechanatstrasse, HfK Bremen

N
W ···▷ ◁··· E
S

use it or lose it

Benutze es
oder
verliere es

love the one
you're with

don't mortgage
the future
building on
dreams

Liebe den Menschen,
mit dem du
zusammen bist

Nimm keine
Hypothek auf
die Zukunft auf,
baue nicht
auf Träume

paradiddles
triplets
syncopation
rhythm
use of space
contrast
control

design is a journey

enjoy being there

Design ist eine Reise

Genieße es,
da zu sein

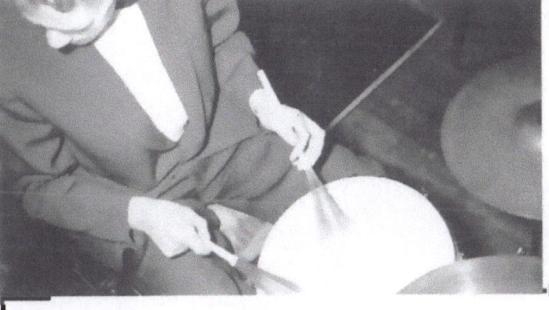

what goes up must come down
Aufstieg auf der Leiter:
Die Sprosse
Die Stufe
Die Spaiche in einem Rad,
Der Zahn in einem Zahnrad,
Wenn Du aufsteigst,
erinnere Dich,
daß Du wider hinunter mußt.

healthy living:
eat three fruits
a day

less fat more life

apples aren't the
only fruit

healthy living:
Iß drei Früchte
am Tag

weniger Fett
mehr Leben

Äpfel sind
nicht die
einzigen Früchte

what goes up must come down
climbing the ladder:
the step
the stair
the step in a wheel,
the tooth in a cog,
a ratchet
reaching higher
on the way up remember
you will need
a hand down

I seem to
specialise in a
creative build-up
which involves
not starting on
the journey but
preparing
everything

I can think of
to avoid
the inevitable:

'creativity is the
successful
resolution of
internal conflicts'.

Ich spezialisiere
mich auf einen
kreativen Aufbau,
der nicht den
Beginn der Reise
sondern die
Vorbereitung von
allem, was mir
einfällt, um das

Unvermeidliche
zu vermeiden,
involviert:
„Kreativität ist
die erfolgreiche
Auflösung
innerer
Konflikte."

when things get
heavy get a lift,
take a taxi

Wenn das Leben
schwer wird,
nimm ein Taxi

reminders: things to pack
Merkhilfen: Dinge, die man einpacken muß

things I must take with me
Dinge, die ich mitnehmen muß

luck: risk informed by experience
Glück: Risiko profitiert von Erfahrung

intuition: instinct informed by luck
Intuition: Instinkt profitiert von Glück

Mood Indigo
by Billy Strayhorn
The Ellington Orchestra
Piano Duke Ellington
Alto sax Johnny Hodges

humility:
seeing Duke Ellington holding the
music, written by Billy Strayhorn,
for Johnny Hodges to play

Demut:
zu sehen wie Duke Ellington
die Noten der Musik von Billy Strayhorn
für Johnny Hodges hält

Über: Suche
on: seeking
nach dem
peace of mind
inneren Frieden

midnight hour blues

In the wee midnight hours
Not quite the break of day

In the wee midnight hours
Not quite the break of day
When the blues creep upon you
and carry your mind away

While I lay in my bed
And cannot go to sleep

While I lay in my bed
And cannot go to sleep
Why my heart's in trouble
And my mind is thinking deep

My mind is running
Back to days of long ago

My mind is running
Back to days of long ago
And the one I love
I don't see her anymore

Blues why do you worry me
Why do you stay so long

Blues why do you worry me
Why do you stay so long
You come to me yesterday
Stayed with me all night long

I've been so worried
I didn't know what to do

I've been so worried
I didn't know what to do

So I guess that's why
I've got these midnight hour blues

Midnight hour blues
Leroy Carr and Scrapper
Blackwell NY 1932

achtung:
(pr's Umschreibung eines Kommentars
von Carl Jung über das Individuum und
die Gesellschaft, die pr. vor 30 Jahren
verloren hat und nicht wiederfinden kann.)
Die Gesellschaft bewundert und braucht
das Streben der Menschheit nach
Individualität. Wenn sie Individualität
gefunden hat, nimmt sie sie auf,
institutionalisiert sie solange bis nichts
mehr von dem vorhanden ist, was sie
einmal wertvoll gemacht hat.

(Zeit, wegzugehen und
einen neuen Tag zu erleben)

warning:
(pr's paraphrase of a Carl Jungian
commentary on the individual and society
which pr lost 30 years ago and cannot
re-find) society praises and needs
the individual spirit of mankind, and when
it finds one it takes it in, institutionalises
it until it can no longer perform in the
manner which once made it valuable.

(Time to walk away
to live again for another day)

On equality
Über Gleichheit
and cultural
und kulturelle
divides
Unterschiede

Black and blue

Cold empty bed
springs all like lead
feel like old ned
wished I was dead

What did I do
to be so black and blue?

Even the mouse
ran from my house
Fell in love with you
and scorned me too

What did I do
to be so black and blue?

I'm white inside
that don't help my case
'cause I can't hide
what is in my face

How will it end
ain't got a friend
My only sin is in my skin
What did I do
to be so black and blue?

My only sin is in my skin
What did I do
to be so black and blue?

Black and Blue
performed by
Louis Armstrong

letter from Jounieh, Lebanon
storm in a tea cup

We had a small drama this morning, happened in front of my sleepy eyes around 6 am, in that dark early morning light which is less than halfway between night and day, more night than early day. This was the same sort of time I used to venture forth on my bicycle to ride to the top of Wimbledon Hill, South London, to deliver newspapers. The sun was trying not too successfully to push its way through the layers of night cloud and in this case sheets of rain. ■ I pulled back the curtains which covered the wall-sized patio doors facing close up the sea across my terrace. Looking over and past the palm trees which had spent all night swaying and flexing under a great storm. This had now subsided in the air but not in the sea which was folding itself into major waves. ■ We are in Jounieh, Lebanon, 1996 at my apartment in the complex of chalets called Amwaj, the Waves. From my balcony, the terrace, at Amwaj, I looked at the amwaj for nearly an hour watching the ocean roll in under the storm clouds from the horizon hundreds of miles, thousands of kilometres, far away. How far is far, I wondered. To know when how far is too far is the sign of genius said Jean Cocteau. ■ What, where, when, why, how are the waves coming. I started counting as I had done at Big Sur waiting for the seventh wave, the big one, the one to ride, wondering, trying to prove really that the seventh wave worked here

on the opposite side of the globe. ■ My eye was distracted in this early misty light breaking through the spray thrown up by the rain. The large curving sweep of the jetty came out from the land at the left in a crescent. Reaching out into the sea, like a protective arm sheltering all the little fishing boats which were now becoming visible. Beyond the curve, the shadowy swell was bobbing up and down restlessly. ■ When the weather was like this in Wimbledon, first up in the morning, the paper shop glowed with the light of an old oil lamp and a paraffin heater around which the paperboys gathered. Printer's ink smelled strongly and the morning frost was on our bikes leaning outside against the brick wall in the alley way. The shop owner's wife gave us hot tea to warm our hands. ■ The two little fishing boats appeared out of the protected harbour heading for the sea. Small boats. More like steep sided rowing boats. In the dim light I could just see three or four dark blobs in each boat; a person at the front, a pile of nets behind, a night light in the centre, a person at the stern, an outboard motor at the back. ■ Today was one of the wettest, windiest mornings. The windswept rainswept mornings which make paperboys think they'd be better off staying in bed. That, I think, is what the fisher-men in the second boat about to leave the shelter of the crescent arm were probably thinking. Or if this was not their first thought they were soon thinking this a little later when

their outboard motor surprised them. It had stopped. ■ Coincidentally I had been wondering why fishermen in general would go out and about in weather such as this. Obviously, I thought, like we had, they had to get the fish delivered. Well collected, then delivered. ■ The first boat had ridden along on all the middle numbers and passed by to disappear towards the horizon. ■ Closer to home the second boat had been puttering along, approaching the harbour exit and making for the sea. I had been counting the waves. This time I was right. Along was coming a really good seventh one. Boat number two was timing its exit nicely to catch this magnificent seventh when its engine stopped. The swell started to wash the boat back out of the way of THE wave but towards the rocks and headland just beyond my palm trees. ■ Which is why I was trying to remember my semaphore, did I mention that earlier? Do they read semaphore in English, French or Arabic? And what was 'do you need help?' 'have you a radio on board?' 'Can you swim? I hope so, as you may need to!' ■ Two oars appeared, one on each side. Frantic rowing took place and the boat seemed to stand still. I remember one of the world's best-known designers telling me that having fallen into teaching in his later years that he felt he was rowing endlessly upstream and only standing still. The boat stood still for quite a time. Not still, but up and down, side to side, around in a spiral.

the team and
images from the
Battle of Words
audio visual production:
by the ndu team lebanon
on 'understanding
a polyglot country',
for profile intermedia 1

Busily going nowhere. I practised my semaphore in front of the mirror but I couldn't reliably get past 'G'. ■ So I did what I'd always been taught to do in a crisis and put the kettle on for a pot of tea. And that did the trick. The next moment I looked, the boat had disappeared and, I think, had made its way back to safety. Just a storm in a tea cup after all.

■ Time to go to work.

Briefe aus dem Jenseits
Brief aus Jounieh, Libanon
Sturm im Teeglas

Heute morgen spielte sich ein kleines Drama ab, direkt vor meinen müden Augen gegen 6 Uhr früh, im dunklen frühen Morgenlicht, das weniger als zur Hälfte zwischen Nacht und Tag liegt, mehr Nacht als früher Tag ist. Es war ungefähr die gleiche Zeit, um die ich auf meinem Fahrrad den Wimbledon Hill in Süd-London erklomm, um Zeitungen auszuliefern. Die Sonne versuchte mit relativ wenig Erfolg, sich ihren Weg durch die Schichten der Nachtwolken – und in diesem Fall der Regenwände – zu bahnen.

▶ Ich zog die Vorhänge auf, die die großen Balkontüren mit Blick auf das Meer direkt gegenüber meiner Terrasse verdeckten. Ich blickte über und an den Palmen vorbei, die sich die ganze Nacht in einem heftigen Sturm gebogen und gewogen hatten. Die Luft hatte sich inzwischen beruhigt, nicht jedoch das Meer, das sich in riesige Wellen legte. Sie stiegen an und brachen sich an den Felsen, das Meer schob sich bis über den Hafendamm und die Brüstungen

jenseits der Palmen und zu meiner Linken vor. ▶ Ich radelte ungefähr die Hälfte des Berges hoch und hielt Ausschau nach dem Express-Milchwagen, dann hielt ich mich an dessen Rückseite fest, als er an mir vorbeifuhr. Mit einer Hand am Wagen, der Arm fast ausgekugelt, mit der anderen am Lenker, der die Belastung abfing, versuchte ich, mich auf dem Rad zu halten. Als ich fast oben am Berg angekommen war, wurde es langsam hell. Die wenigen Straßenlaternen verblaßten, während die Dunkelheit um mich herum heute morgen zur etwa gleichen Zeit im Libanon schwand. ▶ Wir befinden uns in Jounieh, Libanon, 1996, in meiner Wohnung in der Siedlung, die Amwaj – die Wellen – heißt. Von meinem Balkon in Amwaj schaute ich fast eine Stunde lang den Amwaj zu, dem Meer, das unter den Sturmwolken vom Horizont herkommend hunderte von Meilen, tausende von Kilometern entfernt hereinrollte. Ich fragte mich, wie weit entfernt weit eigentlich ist. Zu wissen, wie weit zu weit ist, sei ein Zeichen für Genialität, sagte Jean Cocteau. ▶ Was, wo, wann, warum, wie kommen die Wellen. Ich begann zu zählen, wie ich es in Big Sur getan hatte, als ich auf die siebte Welle wartete, die große, die Welle, die ich reiten wollte, fragte mich, versuchte zu beweisen, daß die siebte Welle auch hier, auf der anderen Seite der Welt, funktionieren würde.

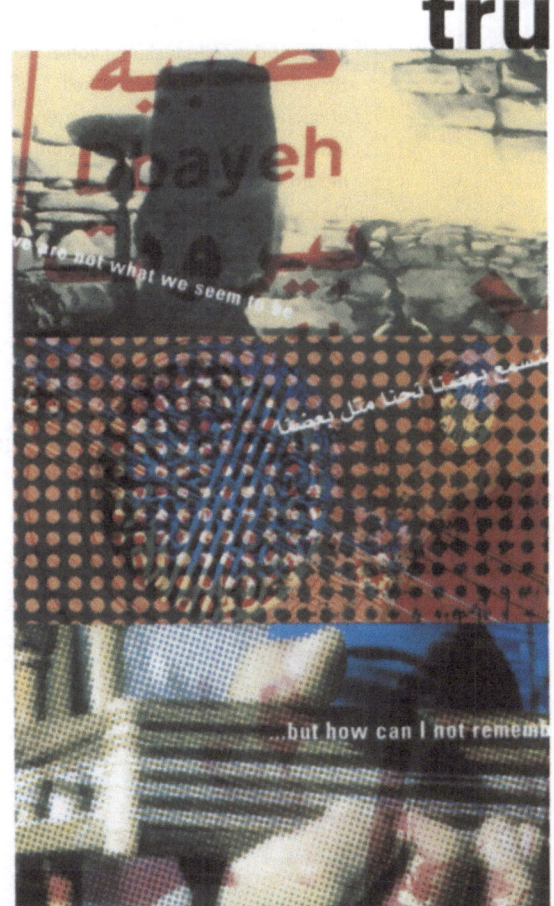

Ich hielt Ausschau nach der größten Welle, die sich in der Morgendämmerung brach, als die beste Welle kam, bildete sich ein neuer Schatten draußen in der Bucht, jenseits des Hafendamms und der Hafenmündung, einige Minuten weit entfernt, der sich beständig, langsam, sicher doch nicht immer verläßlich näherte. Die siebte. Manchmal die neunte. ▶ Mein Auge war in diesem frühen, nebligen Licht, daß durch die vom Regen hochgeworfene Gischt brach, abgelenkt. Der große, gebogene Schwung des Damms löste sich halbmondförmig zu meiner Linken vom Land. Reichte ins Meer hinaus, wie ein beschützender Arm, der die kleinen Fischerboote, die nun sichtbar wurden, umarmte. Jenseits dieser Kurve bewegte sich der schattige Schwall unruhig auf und ab. ▶ Wenn in Wimbledon das Wetter so war und ich ganz früh als Erster aufgestanden war, war der Zeitungsladen vom Schein einer alten Öllampe hell erleuchtet und die Zeitungsjungen standen um eine Paraffin-Heizung herum. Es roch intensiv nach Druckfarbe und der Morgenreif legte sich auf unsere Fahrräder, die wir draußen auf der Straße gegen die Hauswand gelehnt hatten. ▶ Die zwei kleinen Fischerboote verliessen den geschützten Hafen und fuhren – mehr wie Ruderboote – auf die offene See hinaus. In der Dämmerung konnte ich drei bis vier dunkle Kleckse in jedem Boot erkennen: Eine Person stand vorne, dahinter ein Berg von Netzen, eine Lampe und eine Person am Heck, wo sich der Außenbordmotor befand. ▶ Es war ein äußerst nasser und windiger Morgen. Ein so nasser und windiger Morgen, der in jedem Zeitungsjungen

den Wunsch hervorrief, im Bett liegen zu bleiben. Wahrscheinlich war es genau das, was die Männer in dem zweiten Boot in diesem Moment dachten, das gerade den Hafen verließ. Wenn das nicht ihr erster Gedanke war, so muß es zumindest ihr zweiter gewesen sein in dem Moment als ihr Außenbordmotor sie überraschte: Er ging aus. ▶ Ich dachte gerade darüber nach, warum Fischer im allgemeinen bei einem solchen Wetter hinausfuhren. Offensichtlich mussten sie – wie wir damals – den Fisch rechtzeitig ausliefern. Erst fangen und dann ausliefern. ▶ Das erste Boot verschwand gerade am Horizont. ▶ Etwas näher an der Heimat war das zweite Boot damit beschäftigt, den Hafenausgang zu erreichen und in See zu stechen. Ich zählte die Wellen. Dieses Mal hatte ich recht: Die siebte Welle, die soeben nahte, war ziemlich gut. Das zweite Boot erreichte genau rechtzeitig den Hafenausgang, um von dieser Welle erwischt zu werden, als in diesem Moment der Motor aufgab. Die Woge schleuderte das Boot zurück in Richtung der Felsen und landete jenseits der Palmen. ▶ Ich versuchte mich an die Seefahrts-Winkzeichen zu erinnern, die ich einmal gelernt hatte. In welcher Sprache sie wohl Winkzeichen verstanden? Englisch, Französisch oder Arabisch? Und was bedeutete nochmal: »Brauchen Sie Hilfe? Haben Sie ein Funkgerät an Bord? Können Sie schwimmen? Ich hoffe Sie können, denn Sie müssen es wahrscheinlich !« ▶ Jetzt erschienen zwei Ruder. Eines an jeder Seite. Die Fischer begannen hektisch zu rudern, aber das Boot stand still. Ich erinnerte mich an die Worte eines weltberühmten Designers, der in seinen späteren Jahren in die Lehre

gegangen war. Er sagte, daß es ihm so vorkam als rudere er endlos stromauf ohne einen Meter voranzukommen. Das Boot stand eine ganze Weile still, wobei es auf und ab tanzte und sich dabei drehte. Ich übte meine Winkzeichen vor dem Spiegel, aber ich kam nicht weiter als »G«. ▶ Also tat ich, was ich immer in schweren Zeiten tat und setzte einen Kessel mit heißem Wasser auf, um Tee zu kochen. Es funktionierte: Als ich das nächste mal hinausschaute, war das Boot verschwunden. Ich bin mir ganz sicher, dass es den Weg zurück in den sicheren Hafen gefunden hatte: Ein Sturm in der Teetasse zu guter Letzt. ▶ Es ist Zeit zur Arbeit zu gehen.

th

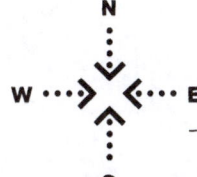

Letter from Germany

Walking across this park started me thinking again. The Bürgerpark is a beautiful park modelled on the German view of English landscaped countryside. Takes me nearly 45 minutes to walk across the narrow dimension. Long views between woodlands across mown and wild fields. Dips, hills, rises in the ground, small irregular lakes and a large symmetrical one on which you can skate in the winter. Gardeners already out. Painting the cast iron seats dark German (and English) racing green against the winter's snow. Repairing the pathway. ■ I passed six or seven homeless people around their sleeping bags under an archway. A dog and a bowl for money if anyone cares. ■ People stand at the kerbs waiting for the traffic lights, which are red, to change to green to cross the empty road. Trams swish quietly along with hardly a sound. And no one asks to see the ticket which you may or may not have. How I wonder: can we compare the work of German designers against the work from war-torn countries and socially different conditions.

Letter from Lebanon, again

This is a country after nearly 20 years of external and internal war and a few years of semi-independence. Rebuilding its architecture, roads, life and its education. ■ Sunday, and a chance to be away from the city. Up the mountain road into the hills. Skies so blue that Winsor and Newton paint or Apple Macintosh couldn't match them. A goatherd shouts out, dogs bark. Sounds of clean air blowing over us, the cock crowing, trilling of the goatherd, a dog barks again. Goat bells ring. Birds. Far down in the valley: occasional traffic noises. Below us the rolling of rrrs and shhhing of the goatherd, a radio, the cock trying harder. For a moment all is silence. Why, one wonders, should current Anglo-Euro-American trends in graphic design be of any interest here? ■ Dynamos and generators keeping the back-up systems running for the computers, the power and the lighting. ■ Our students have no experience doing art and design at junior or high school, not done. We teach from scratch on a wing and a prayer. (En ch allah... if god wills.)

trust_

Brief aus Deutschland

Der Spaziergang durch diesen Park brachte mich erneut ins Grübeln. Der Bürgerpark ist ein schöner Park, aus der deutschen Auffassung der englischen Landschaftsgärten heraus modelliert. Ich brauchte fast 45 Minuten, um die enge Dimension zu durchqueren. Lange Aussichten zwischen Wäldern über gemähte und wildgewachsene Wiesen. Vertiefungen, Hügel, Erhebungen, kleine, unregelmäßige Seen und ein großer, asymmetrischer, auf dem man im Winter Schlittschuh laufen kann, Gärtner bei der Arbeit. Sie streichen die gußeisernen Bänke in deutschem (und englischem) Grün vor der verschneiten, weißen Landschaft. Reparieren den Weg. ▶ Ich kam an sechs oder sieben Obdachlosen vorbei, mit ihren Schlafsäcken unter einem Durchgang. Ein Hund und eine Schüssel - für Geld, sofern das einen berührt. ▶ Menschen stehen am Bürgersteig und warten, daß die rote Ampel auf grün umschaltet, damit sie die leere Straße überqueren können. Straßenbahnen zischen fast lautlos vorbei. Keiner fragt nach der Fahrkarte, die man gekauft hat - oder auch nicht. Wie, so frage ich mich, können wir die Arbeiten von Deutschen Designern mit denen vergleichen, die aus kriegführenden Ländern und einem anderen sozialen Umfeld kommen?

Brief aus dem Libanon (wieder)

Es ist Sonntag und die Gelegenheit, aus der Stadt zu kommen. Die Bergstraße hoch in die Berge. Ein Himmel so blau, daß Winsor oder Newton-Farben oder der Apple Macintosh es nicht wiedergeben könnten. Eine Ziegenherde schreit, Hunde bellen. Klare Luft weht über uns hinweg, der Hahn schreit, das Trillern des Ziegenhirtes, wieder bellt ein Hund. Ziegenglocken klingeln. Vögel. Weit unten im Tal: gelegentliche Verkehrsgeräusche. Unter uns die rollenden Rufe des Hirten, ein Radio, der Hahn bemüht sich zunehmend. Einen Augenblick lang ist alles still. Warum, fragt man sich, sollten aktuelle anglo-europäisch-amerikanische Trends im Grafik-Design hier irgendjemanden interessieren? ▶ Dynamos und Generatoren halten die Backup-Systeme für die Computer, Strom und Licht in Gang. ▶ Unsere Studenten haben keine Erfahrung mit Kunst oder Design in der Realschule oder im Gymnasium — das gibt es nicht. Unser Unterricht beginnt bei den Anfängen, mit einem Stoßgebet auf den Lippen (En ch allah...so Gott will).

Blue skies from mount lebanon
pr 1996

written for :output no.1;
the international year book
for works of graphic design
students: 1998

dream traveller: girl in a diner 1970 USA: pr

road stories

the far side of america

The mustang drove like a black arrow for many hundreds of miles. Looking neither to the left nor to the right. Across Oklahoma prairies and Texas pastures, mesmerised by the great concrete ribbon. The all black fast back jumped and bucked its way round corners, leapt off the road and down into the forgotten mainstreets and crossroads of Steinbeck novels. ■ This life isn't only travelled in straight lines. Many detours, mountains, valleys, sunshine, clouds, rain. ■ Deserts surround the edge of California. Leaving Las Vegas and its cacti of electric signs, exploding mechanical volcanoes, wedding chapels and honeymoon hotels, is one desert to another. The road leads into the Mojave Desert or to Death Valley. Sweltering. Deserted except for Joshua trees and glinting tin boxes buzzing across, racing the sun climbing to the height of the day. Skimming through 120 degree hallucinations to the cool Pacific mountains on the far side. Through this no-man's-land which belongs to the Indians. ■ Two lanes become three, three become four, become six and seven sweeping nonstop until bursting off the San Bernadino Freeway, off the Santa Monica Freeway, through the Santa Monica Arch and there is is the ocean which you couldn't see for three and a half

**my road
1971
america
americar
americana
amerikarma**

Der Mustang fuhr hunderte von Meilen wie ein schwarzer Pfeil. Kein Blick nach rechts oder links. Durch die Prärien in Oklahoma und über texanische Weiden, fasziniert von dem riesigen Band aus Beton. Der „all black fast back" sprang und schlang sich um Kurven, wich von der Straße ab und fuhr über vergessene Hauptstraßen und Kreuzungen aus Steinbeck-Romanen. ▸ Dieses Leben verläuft nicht nur in geraden Linien. Viele Umleitungen, viele Berge, Täler, viel Sonne, Wolken, Regen. ▸ Wüsten umgeben die Ränder Kaliforniens. Las Vegas verlassen und seine Kakteen aus Neonschildern, explodierenden mechanischen Vulkanen, Heiratskapellen und Flitterwochenhotels liegen zwischen zwei Wüsten. Die Straße führt in die Mojave-Wüste oder ins Tal des Todes. Brütende Hitze. Verlassen, außer von den Joshua-Bäumen und den glitzernden Flugzeugen, die über mir vorbeiziehen, im Wettlauf mit der Sonne, die ihrem höchsten Stand näherkommt. Durch 120 Grad-Halluzinationen bis zu den kühlen Bergen am Pazifik am anderen Ende. Durch dieses Niemandsland, das den Indianern gehört. ▸ Aus zwei Spuren werden drei, aus drei werden vier, sechs und sieben, die sich ununterbrochen dahinziehen, bis sie vom San Bernardino Freeway oder vom Santa Monica Freeway ausbrechen. Durch den Santa Monica Arch hindurch – und da ist der Ozean, den man dreieinhalb Tausend Meilen lang nicht sehen konnte. ▸ Einen Strand weit entfernt. Dort, umrahmt

the wild west
1971: pr

turn right to the road not taken: pr
from the poem by Robert Frost

thousand miles. ■A beach a way. There framed in an arch cut through the final mountain range is the other side of America. ■Los Angeles maintains the aura of a set on the film lot, waiting to be struck. For under that city much of the coast line has been reclaimed not from the sea but from the desert. ■Century City, a city within a city, stands complete upon the bygone film lots of 20th Century Fox. This miniature Manhattan of glass and metal is deserted by walking people, populated by automobiles and elevators depositing and collecting their riders who circulate via air conditioned corridors about the business of their city. ■Panned from a distance the panoramic view looks scrubby, sandy, slightly barren and faded. In close-up there is an over abundance of exotic trees, grass, clover and flowering bushes. Usually too many and too much to be true. Everything seems vaguely transient, even the towering palm trees are unbalanced with heavy heads and swaying stems. Since nature, with a fitness for purpose, gives supple stems to plants that may need them. So I wonder whether a transient flexibility is a true Californian quality, required in order to survive this specially unique film-set society of LA.

von einem Bogen, der aus dem letzten Bergrücken geschnitten wurde, liegt die andere Seite von Amerika. Los Angeles hat noch immer die Aura eines Filmsets, und wartet darauf, erwischt zu werden. Denn unter dieser Stadt wurde ein Großteil der Küste nicht vom Meer zurück gefordert, sondern von der Wüste. ▸ Century City, eine Stadt in der Stadt, steht auf den ehemaligen Filmgeländen der Twentieth Century Fox. Dieses Manhattan in Miniaturausgabe aus Glas und Metall wurde von den Fußgängern verlassen und wird jetzt von Autos und Aufzügen, die ihre in klimatisierten Korridoren den Geschäften ihrer Stadt nachgehenden Mitfahrer ausstoßen und einsammeln, bevölkert. ▸ Aus der Ferne betrachtet, sieht das Panorama immer gestrüppreich, sandig, leicht unfruchtbar und verblaßt aus. Aus der Nähe gesehen, gibt es hier einen Überfluß an exotischen Bäumen, Gras, Klee und blühenden Büschen. Gewöhnlich zu viele und zu übertrieben, um wahr zu sein. Alles scheint vergänglich zu sein, selbst die Palmen sehen mit ihren schweren Köpfen und wankenden Stämmen so aus, als hätten sie das Gleichgewicht verloren. Da die Natur mit ihrem Sinn für einen Zweck den Pflanzen, die sie benötigen könnten, biegsame Stämme verleiht, frage ich mich, ob eine vergängliche Flexibilität eine wahre kalifornische Eigenschaft ist, die man braucht, um in dieser besonders einzigartigen Filmset-Gesellschaft von Los Angeles überleben zu können.

cherokee lake: pr
on the road less travelled by

my life as a designer-teacher

has always incurred lengthy physical journeys

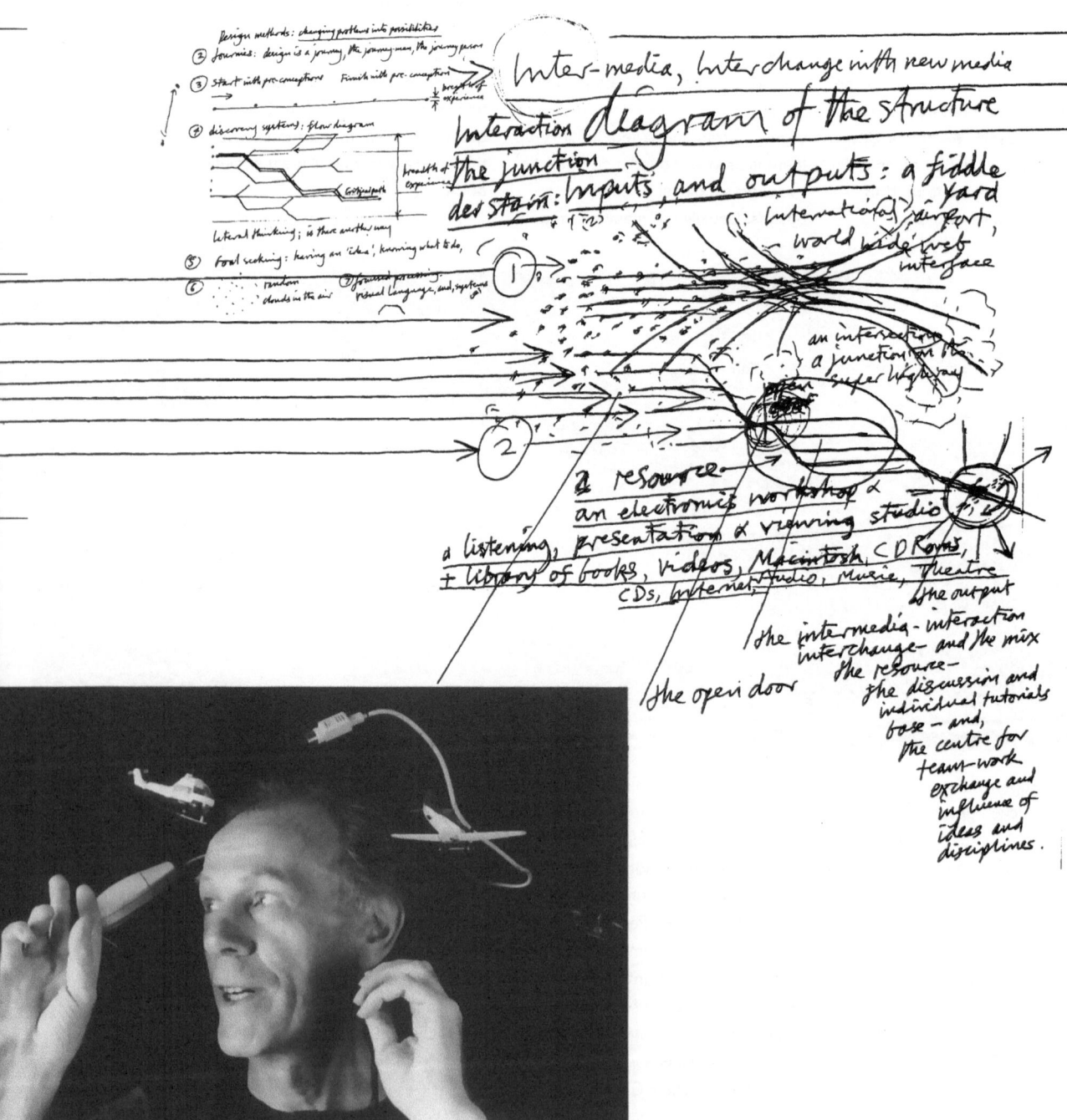

homage to Rodchenko's:
poet talking to his tax inspector;
pr photo by Jacky Chapman 1996

I can be sitting in my London garden talking to my friends on a hands-free phone while they are travelling down the highway in Beirut, halfway up a mountain or walking in the Mitte in Berlin. Email and fax make nonsense of any sense of scale and distance. The concept of the world is changing. Time is how distance is measured. Everyone is a next-door neighbour.

■ Let's meet at 'My place' is not always the same place now that I've reorganised my map of the world.

Ich kann in meinem Garten in London sitzen und mit meinen Freunden an einem Handy sprechen, die sich gerade auf der Autobahn in Beirut befinden oder in Berlin Mitte. E-mail und Fax machen Größe und Entfernungen sinnlos. Das Konzept der Welt verändert sich. Entfernungen werden nach der Zeit gemessen. Jeder Mensch ist ein Nachbar.

▸ »Wir treffen uns bei mir«, ist nicht mehr der gewohnte Ort, jetzt, nachdem ich die Weltkarte neu gezeichnet habe.

W
S ···▸ ▸ ◂··· N
E

the compass
junction of the way's
choice: the road less
travelled by
wahl
destiny
schicksal
karma
kismet
kiss
met

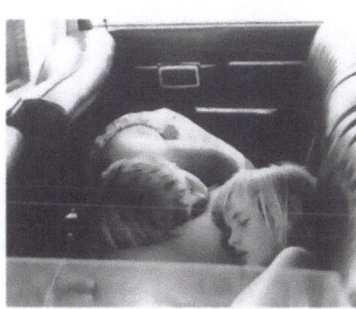

the sun which rises in the east sets in the west

travelling letters

9 June 1999.
Ich sitze im ICE. Ich reise mit 280 km/h und »Zeitlos Dawn« ist an den Strom angeschlossen. Noch 6 Stunden bis nach Bremen.

»Zeitlos Dawn« – mein Powerbook – funktioniert gut. Ich habe gerade meine Vorlesung „Erinnerungen sind wie Tränen im Regen" beendet. Meine Notizen sind verwischt. Die Tinte ist verlaufen. Aber wohin ist sie verschwunden?

Was sind Erinnerungen ohne Gefühl. Warum kann ich mich nicht erinnern, wenn ich vergesse? Sind Tränen unauslöschlich? Sie sind die Patina des Lebens. Wohin gehen Tränen, wenn sie verschwinden.

Draußen hinter der Scheibe: Schnelle Reise in die Vergangenheit. Blauer Himmel füllt die Löcher zwischen den Wolken. Sonnenstrahlen füllen den Raum zwischen den Schatten.

Erinnerungen sind die Löcher im Universum. Sie warten darauf, mit Bedeutung gefüllt zu werden. Zeichen sind wie ein leeres Glas, das darauf wartet, gefüllt zu werden. Wittgenstein.

Augen sind wie tiefe Löcher, in denen man nach Weisheit tauchen kann. Figur und Grund warten darauf, vereinigt zu werden. In meinem Kopf: Pläne, Flugzeuge, Ebenen, Berge, Dörfer, Seen, Himmel, Augen.

9 June 1999.
Sitting on the ICE train. Germany. Zeitlos Dawn plugged into their power supply travelling at 280 km per hour. Six hours to Bremen.

Zeitlos Dawn, timeless tomorrow, my powerbook, is working well. I've just finished 'memories are like tear drops in the rain'. Blurred my notes. The ink ran. But where did it run to?

What are memories without emotion. If I am to forget how may I not remember? Are tear drops indelible? They are the patina of life. If memories fade away, where do they fade to?

Outside my window: travelling past, fast. Blue skies filling the holes between clouds. Sunbeams filling the spaces between shadows. Memories are holes in the universe waiting to be filled with meaning.

Signs are like an empty glass waiting to be filled. Wittgenstein.

Eyes are like deep pools to be dived in, seeking for wisdom. Figure and ground waiting to be joined.

Inside my mind: plans, planes, plains, mountains, villages, seas, skies, eyes.

end of a journey
mad and reb
photo: J9

NORTH/LONDON

070 TO 095

Founded in 1995 by Simon Browning and Sean Perkins, the London-based design group North follows a resolutely dynamic approach to graphic design. The nine-person team is a progressive contrast to large, traditional »British« corporate identity companies.

THE PURSUIT OF A RESOLUTELY MODERN AND EUROPEAN APPROACH TO GRAPHIC DESIGN.
THESE PAGES ARE A COLLABORATION OF FASHION PHOTOGRAPHER AMBER ROWLANDS AND NORTH.

Die 1995 von Simon Browning und Sean Perkins gegründete Design-gruppe North mit Sitz in London verfolgt einen entschieden dynamischen Ansatz des Grafik Design. Das neunköpfige Team stellt einen progressiven Kontrast zu den großen, traditionellen »britischen« Corporate Identity-Unternehmen dar.

DIE DURCHSETZUNG EINES MODERN RESOLUTEN UND EUROPÄISCHEN ANSATZES IM GRAFIK DESIGN.
DIESE SEITEN SIND EINE ZUSAMMEN-ARBEIT DER MODEFOTOGRAFIN AMBER ROWLANDS UND NORTH.

Juergen
Teller
29 May
25 July
The
Photographe
Gallery
Great Newport Street

ers'

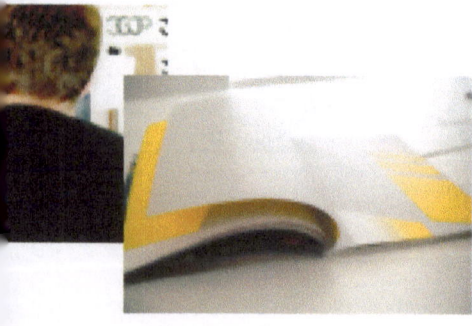

MAIRA & TIBOR KALMAN / NEW YORK

096 TO 119

Maira and Tibor Kalman collaboratively worked on a wide variety of projects from their New York studio M&Co (the »M« stands for Maira). In 1993 Oliviero Toscani offered to run »Colors« from Rome; they closed M&Co, sold most of it in a gigantic yard sale, and off the Kalmans moved to Italy. Shattering the conventions of good taste and order, the work of both communicates through the power of humor, the vernacular, and an »upside-down« thinking.
(TRANSLATION ON PAGE 220)

YOUR CULTURE (WHOEVER YOU ARE) IS AS IMPORTANT AS OUR CULTURE (WHOEVER WE ARE). TIBOR KALMAN WAS EDITOR OF THE FIRST THIRTEEN ISSUES OF THE BENETTON MAGAZINE COLORS. HE DIED ON MAY 2ND 1999.

Maira und Tibor Kalman arbeiteten gemeinsam an einer großen Bandbreite von Projekten in ihrem New Yorker Studio M&Co (das »M« steht für Maira). 1993 bot Oliviero Toscani an, direkt in Rom an »Colors« zu arbeiten; M&Co wurde geschlossen, ein Großteil des Inventars verkauft, und die Kalmans zogen nach Italien. Indem sie die Konventionen des guten Geschmacks und der Ordnung durchbrechen, wirken die Arbeiten der beiden durch die Kraft des Humors, das Derbe und das »auf den Kopf gestellte Denken«.
(ÜBERSETZUNG AUF SEITE 220)

EURE KULTUR (WER IMMER IHR SEID) IST EBENSO WICHTIG WIE UNSERE KULTUR (WER AUCH IMMER WIR SIND). TIBOR KALMAN WAR HERAUSGEBER DER ERSTEN DREIZEHN AUSGABEN DES BENETTON MAGAZINS COLORS. ER STARB AM 2. MAI 1999.

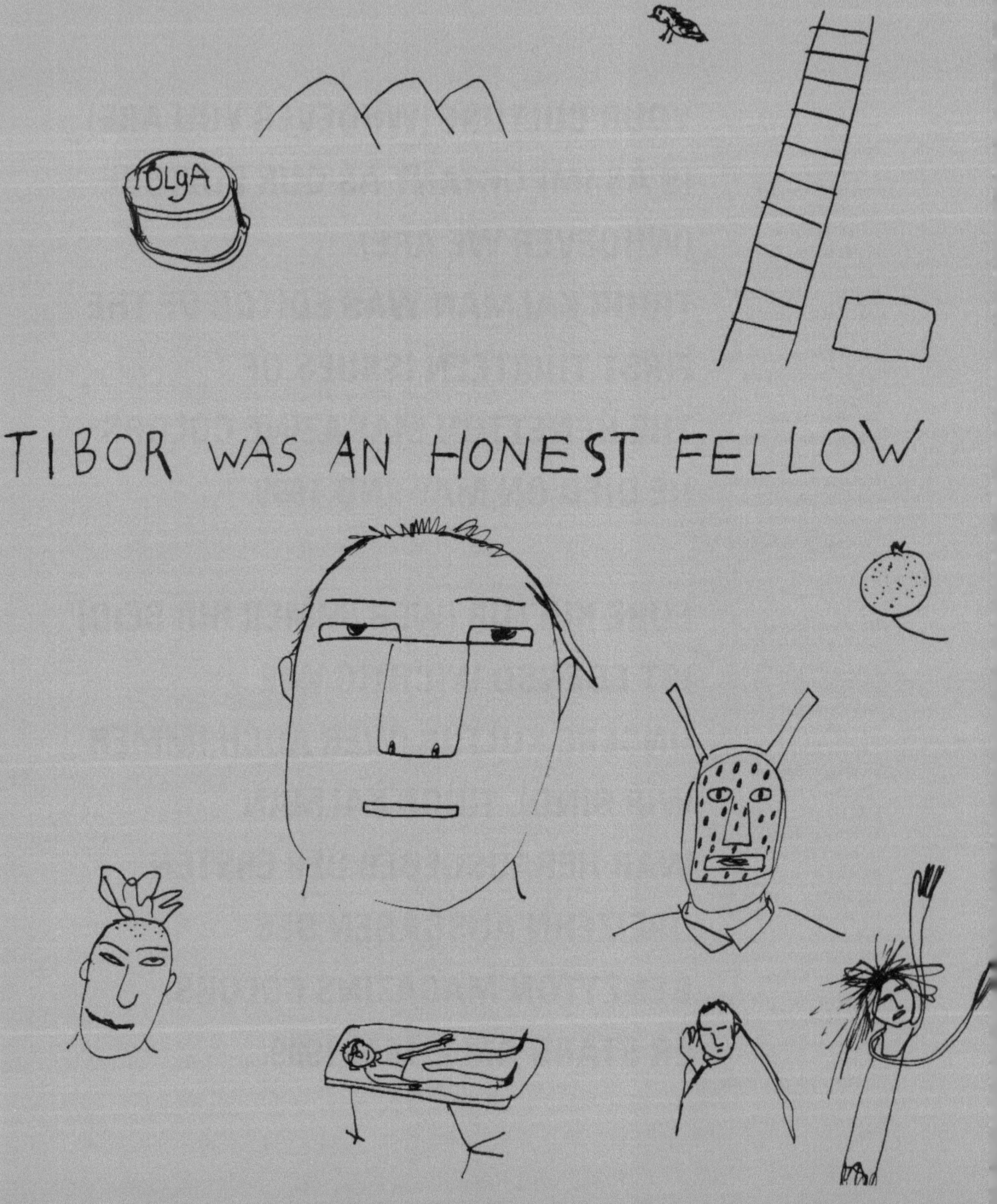

TIBOR WAS AN HONEST FELLOW

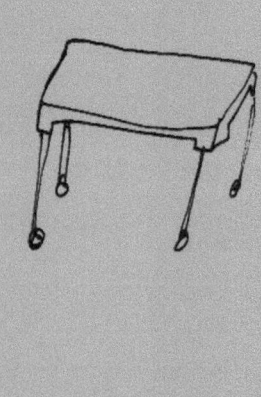

BRILLIANT FUNNY AND WISE

COMPLETELY INCONCEIVABLE
THAT HE IS NO LONGER
HERE.

IMPOSSIBLE.

M. KALMAN
NOVEMBER 1999

»Over the years, there's a lot of talk about the planet becoming »smaller«
that technology wether it's the jet plane or fax machine or communications
satellite, is erasing the differences between cultures and peoples.
We don't think this should be the case. The message of this magazine is
that your culture (whoever you are) is as important as our culture
(whoever we are). We think that the real value of all the electronic stuff
that creates links between places otherwise completely removed
from each other is that it allows all of us to see further and broaden our
ways of thinking. We want to know what you're doing over there
(wherever you are), and we're pretty sure you want to know what we're
doing here (wherever we are).« *Colors No. 1, It's a Baby, Fall/Winter 1991*

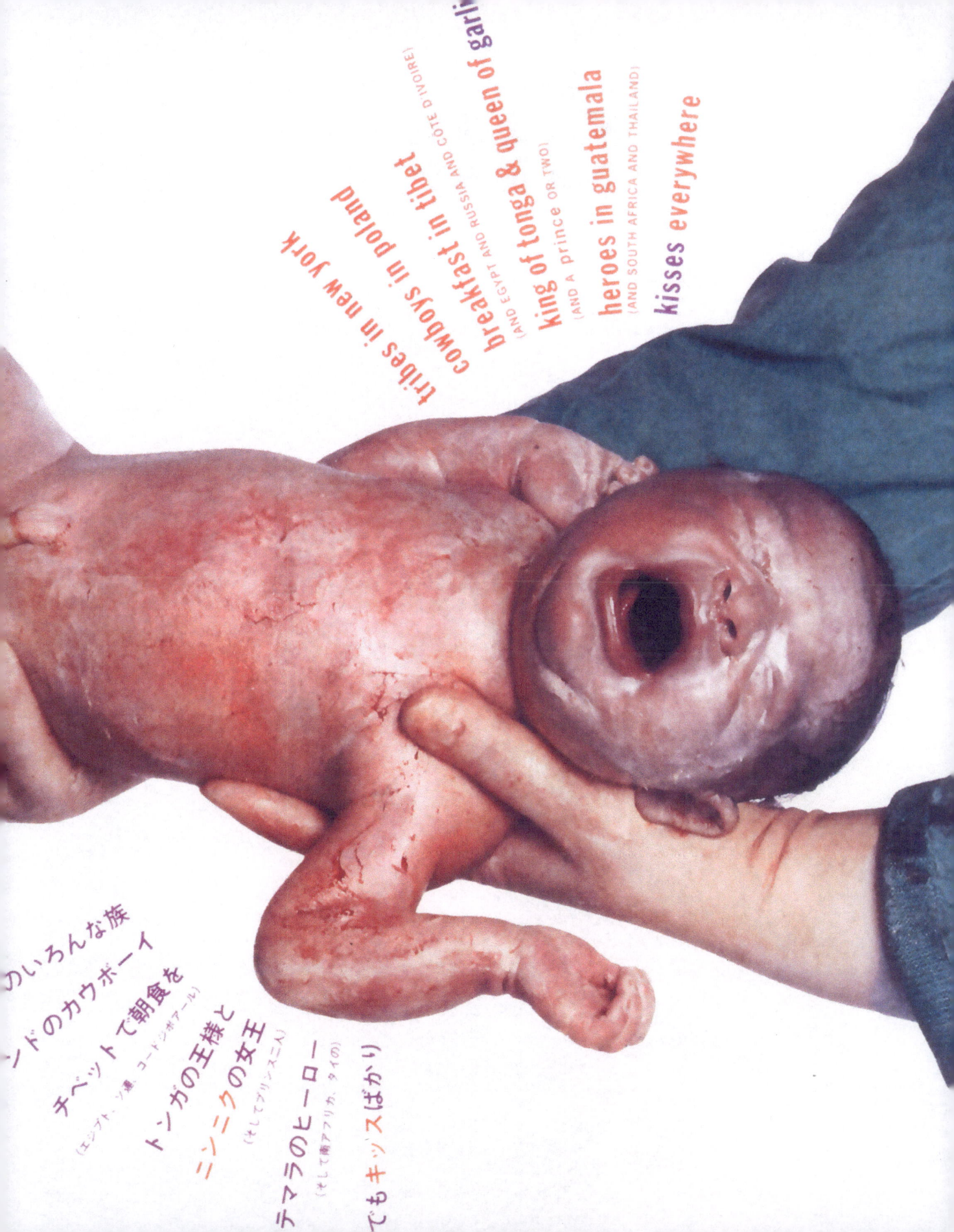

tribes in new york
cowboys in poland
breakfast in tibet (AND EGYPT AND RUSSIA AND CÔTE D'IVOIRE)
king of tonga & queen of garlic (AND A PRINCE OR TWO)
heroes in guatemala (AND SOUTH AFRICA AND THAILAND)
kisses everywhere

ンドのいろんな族

ンドのカウボーイ

チベットで朝食を
(エジプト、ソ連、コートジボアール)

トンガの王様と
ニンニクの女王
(そしてプリンスニ人)

テマラのヒーロー
(そして南アフリカ、タイの)

でもキッスは（ばかり）

dio?

what if..?
¿qué pasaría si..?

Queen Elizabeth
La reina Isabel

The **STREET** is where people stroll,
hurry, ask directions, wait for lovers,
stop for food, run into friends, walk home . . .
or just barely survive.
It's where we went to search for
heroes.

Auf der **STRASSE** gehen Menschen spazieren, eilen,
fragen nach dem Weg, warten auf Liebhaber,
halten zum Essen an, treffen Freunde, gehen nach Hause ...
oder überleben gerade so.
Dort suchten wir nach
Helden.

SANDRA LIMA SILVA
(top right) watches over
her girls on a Rio street.
SANDRA LIMA SILVA
(oben rechts) paßt auf
einer Straße in Rio auf
ihre Mädchen auf.

Ich habe Angst, vergewaltigt zu werden. Das ist, wenn ein Mann dich packt, in den Wald schleppt und dir wehtut. –Priscila Maria Coelho da Costa, 7 Jahre

I'm afraid of being raped. That's when a man grabs you and takes you off to the woods and hurts you. –Priscila Maria Coelho da Costa, age 7

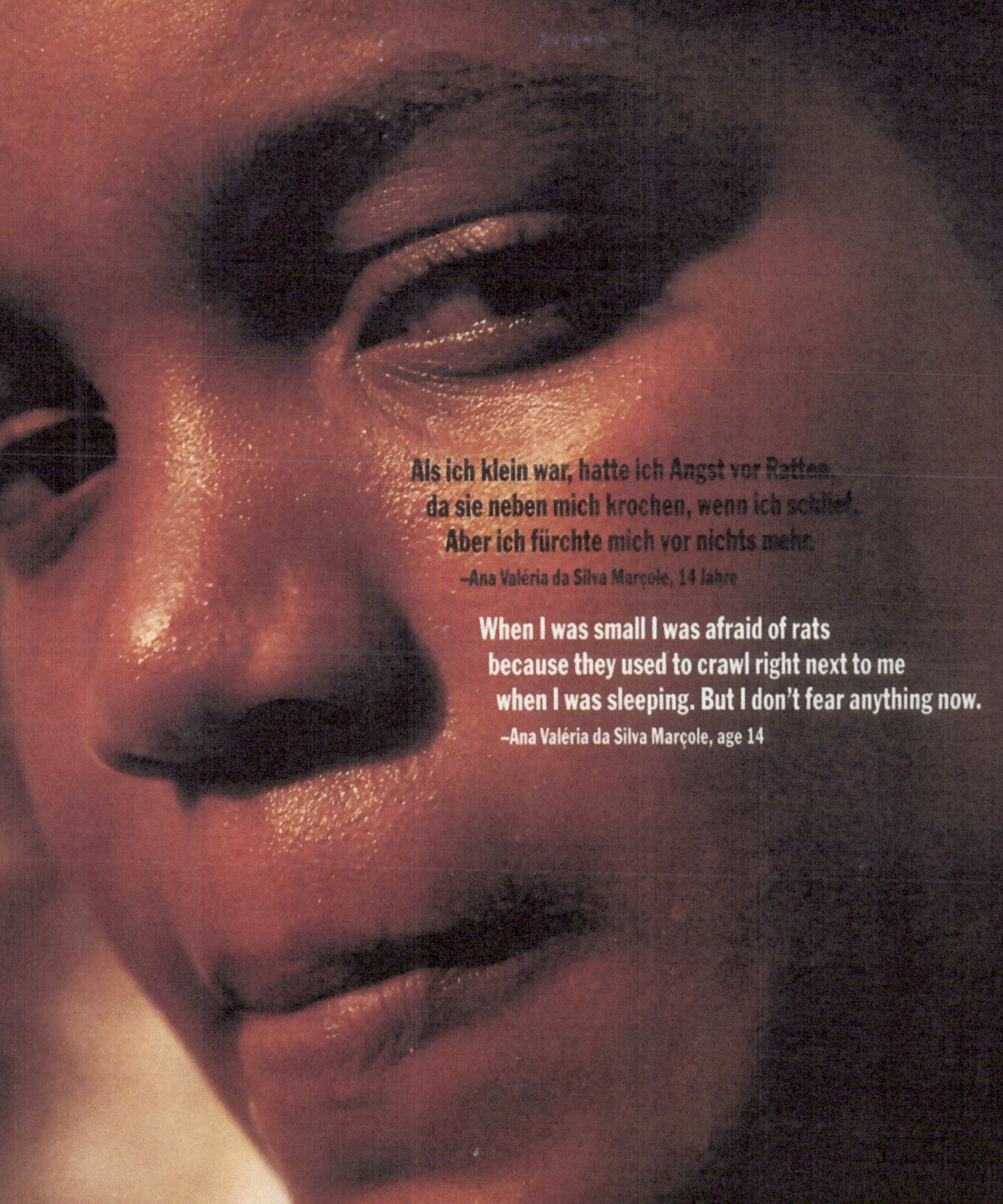

Als ich klein war, hatte ich Angst vor Ratten,
da sie neben mich krochen, wenn ich schlief.
Aber ich fürchte mich vor nichts mehr.
—Ana Valéria da Silva Marçole, 14 Jahre

When I was small I was afraid of rats
because they used to crawl right next to me
when I was sleeping. But I don't fear anything now.
—Ana Valéria da Silva Marçole, age 14

as usual, this magazine
wie üblich landet die

ends up in the garbage.
ses Magazin im Müll

Ten square meters of tropical rainforest
are consumed by every hamburger produced
in Central America.

the future
of medicine

the cure for AIDS is likely to be in this picture.
we haven't found it yet.
if we don't hurry, the picture might disappear

"I have lost 77 friends
since December 26, 1991."

"Am meisten stört mich,
dass ich kein Obst und Gemüse
mehr essen kann."

I can't imagine
being gone.

"The constant cheeriness
of doctors and nurses drives
me insane."

"Seit dem 26. Dezember
1991 habe ich 77 Freunde
verloren."

"Ich habe jede Menge Schulden.
Die muss ich nicht bezahlen.
Zur Hölle mit dem BAFöG !"
"What bothers me most is giving up fruits and vegetables."
"Die penetrant gute Laune der Ärzte und Schwestern macht mich verrückt."
"Ich kann mir nicht vorstellen, nicht mehr da zu sein."
"I owe all kinds of money. I'm never going to have to pay it back. Screw those student loans!"

MICHAEL SAUP / FRANKFURT

120 _{TO} 139

Ranging among different artistic forms of expression, the installation R111 is a reference to a film by Oskar Fischinger called »R-1« – a film which comes out of the beginnings of the art of animation. Fischinger's exploration of the interaction between sound and image in film have supplied a historical stimulus for this installation by Michael Saup and his group Supreme Particles. (TRANSLATION ON PAGE 220)

THE INSTALLATION R111 INVESTIGATES THE CIRCULATION OF VIRTUAL ENERGY CURRENTS AND INDUCES THE TRANSFORMATION FROM DIGITAL INFORMATION TO ANALOGUE MATTER.

Zwischen verschiedenen künstlerischen Darstellungsformen bezieht sich die Installation R111 auf den Film »R-1« von Oskar Fischinger aus den Anfängen der Animationskunst. Fischingers Erforschung des Zusammenspiels von Ton und Bild im Film sind ein historischer Impulsgeber für diese Arbeit von Michael Saup und seiner Gruppe Supreme Particles. (ÜBERSETZUNG AUF SEITE 220)

DIE INSTALLATION R111 UNTERSUCHT DEN KREISLAUF VIRTUELLER ENERGIESTRÖME UND LEITET DIE TRANSFORMATION VON DIGITALER INFORMATION IN ANALOGE MATERIE EIN.

R111

aufbruch

die installation R111 ist
eine räumliche anordnung
von verschiedenen
materiellen, immateriellen,
visuellen, akustischen
und taktilen repräsentationen
eines energetischen systems.

aggression

unterschiedliche »virtuelle aggregatzustände«

manipulieren läßt das gesamtsystem.

und die interaktion der benutzer/innen

sowie der stete elektronische datentransfer

führen ihm energie zu. diese verwandlung

von daten- und energieströmen wird

bei R... an den algorithmen eines com-

pu...

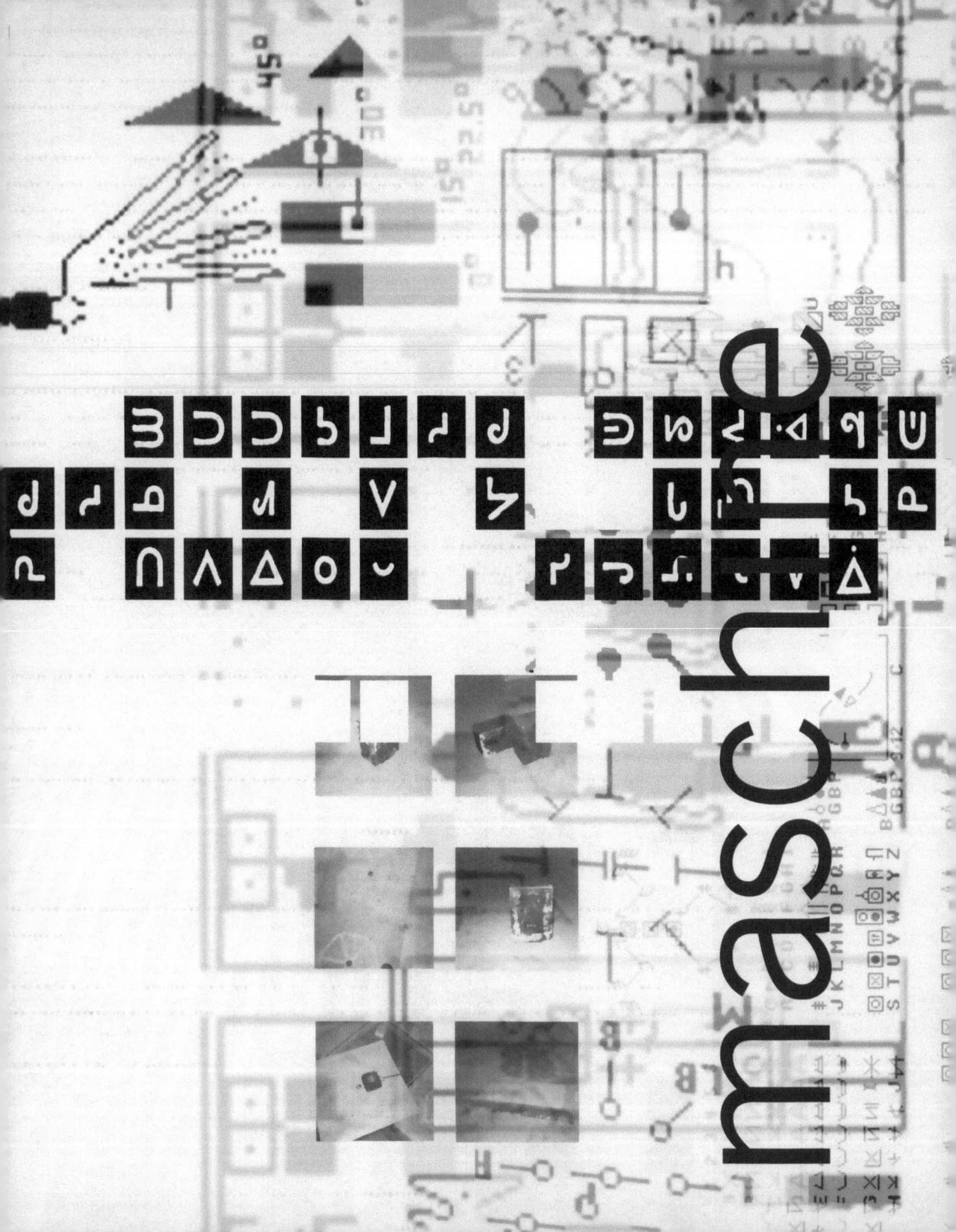

auflösung

die bewegungen der besucher/innen und
eingespeiste daten aus dem netz steuern
den animationen zugrundeliegende
programm. als benutzer-interface fungiert
dabei eine durch ein motion-tracking-system
gesteuerte bodenplatte (soundfloor), die
energie (bewegung) aufnimmt. sie repräsentiert die schnittstelle zwischen der analogen
und der digitalen welt von R111.

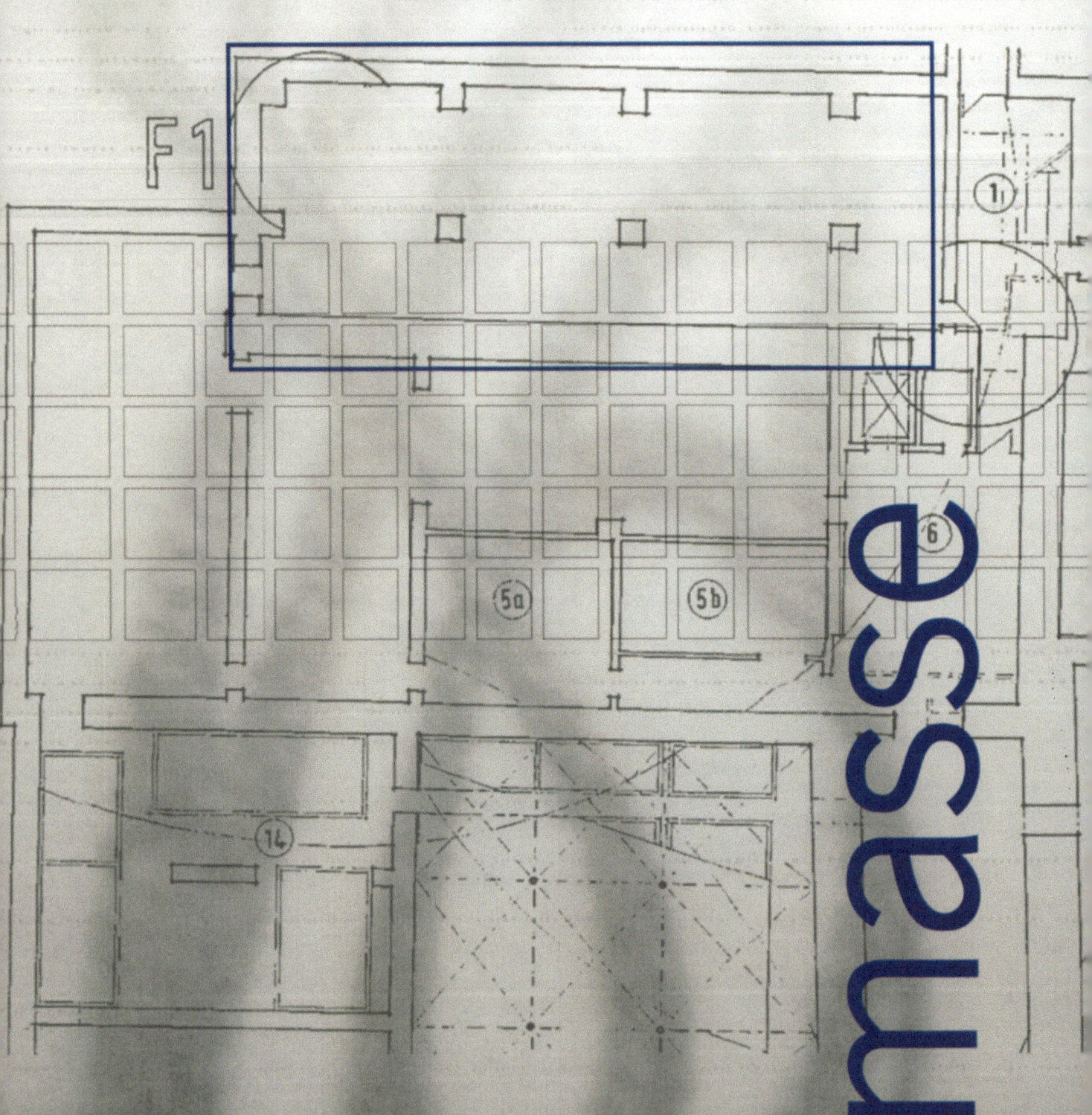

abstraktion

ein großes „R" bezeichnet die halle als das herz der installation. der raum repräsentiert die „virtuelle welt" des systems, das in einer anderen halle in seinem teilaspekt etwa als „in der zeit gefrorene materie" gezeigt wird.

R

mono:

anti.

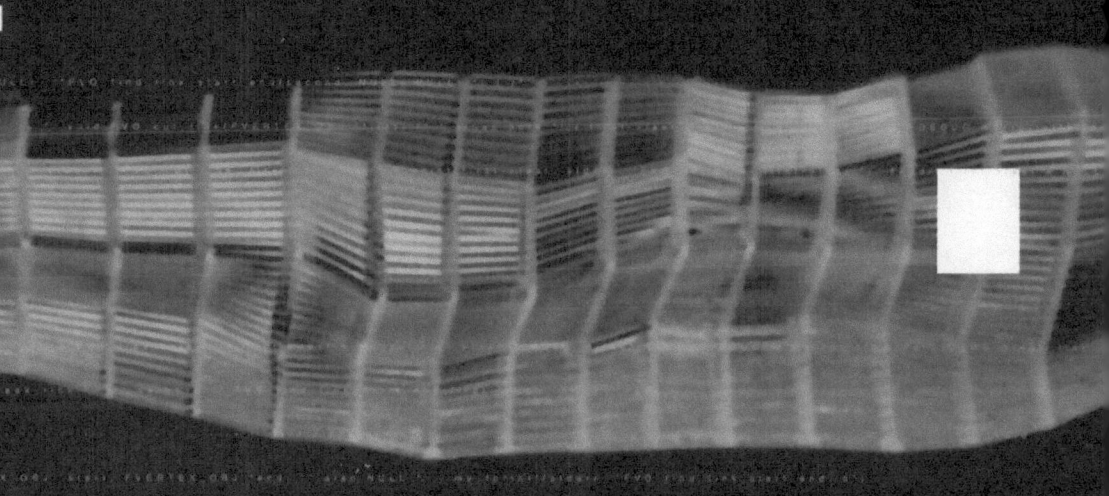

anne niemetz anna saup adrian saup
felix saup gideon may steina vasulka
charly steinberg stefan karp bob
o'kane dieter sellin kai guse fritz
deutschland peter weibel michael
simon heiner goebbels ballett
frankfurt decoi lostinspace phil
dadson adrian croucher darryn
harkness shane currey mike hodgson
chris gee dj tricky cris herbert
cybulska constanze ruhm kay fricke
peter sandbichler julian boyd dan
powell cornelia franke paul modler
richard castelli epidemic art zoyd
pierre vasseur elektrolux boso söke
dinkla katharina gsöllpointner arnd
wesemann steffen cramer gerhard
stäbler dr. scissors timo piatkowski
armin purkrabek stefan hofmann jan
totzek marc kaiser lars werbeck

angst

in den nächsten räumen dominieren verweise auf weitere materielle und
immaterielle aggregatzustände: desolate materie (stein- und mauerbrocken)
neben elektronischer hardware als schnittstelle zum world wide web,
materialisierte töne oder im konzept von supreme particles dort angesiedelte
granulare materie

atom

als crossover-arbeit zwischen verschiedenen künstlerischen darstel-lungsformen bezieht sich die installation auf eine arbeit aus den anfängen der animationskunst. den film „R-1" von oskar fischinger, den der deutsche künstler 1927 produziert hat. fischinger, der neben experimenten mit konkreten

und „absoluten" film-animationen vor allem auch das zusammenspiel von ton und bild im film erforschte. ist ein historischer impulsgeber für die installation von supreme particles. R111 bezieht sich auf „R-1" und verweist damit auch auf esoterische bezugspunkte – im sinne religiöser

und/oder nur für eingeweihte zugäng-licher information, die es sowohl bei fischinger gab, als auch beim virtuel-len system von supreme particles. es kann hier etwa auf 111 als die zahl sieben im binären darstellungssystem verwiesen werden usw.

matrix

apathie

gleichzeitig erinnert die installation nicht nur im titel an francois truffauts film „fahrenheit 451" (i.e. netscape 451) von 1966, einen sozialkritischen science fiction klassiker, der die subversiven möglichkeiten individueller widerstände gegen machtstrukturen zum inhalt hat. truffauts filmtitel (nach einem roman von ray bradbury) bezieht sich auf jene temperatur, bei der die bücher verbrennen. und benennt damit den übergang von einem aggregatzustand von materie in einen anderen.

die vielseitigen verweise und assoziationen bei R1?1 machen die arbeit über ihre interaktive und visuelle präsentation hinaus zu einer abhandlung über die offenheit von systemen und die stete interferenz von energie und materie (information).

molekül

A

src->att_dist; dst->max_att_dist < src->max_att_dist; dst->n_att_dist< src->n_att_dist;

< src->de___; dst->max_d___dist   < src->max_decay_dist; dst->n_decay_dist   < src->n_decay_dist;

src->velo, dst->   src->mass; dst->drag   < src->drag;

< s->velo   < src->velo; dst->acc   < src->acc; dst->dt   < src->dt;

w ize grow '/ dst->grow   < src->grow/* 0 '1 '/ dst->grow_dt < src->grow_dt;] /*---------------------------------'/ void FVO_---

src_ gx(FVERTEX_OBJ 'src, FVERTEX_OBJ 'dst) { dst->abgr   < src->abgr; dst->c_interp   < src->c_interp; dst->smooth   < src->smooth; dst->tc< src

d; dst_   < src->tex_id; dst->env_id   < src->lines;   < src->lines;

src->abgr_mapped   < src->abgr_mapped;) /*--'/ void FVO_copy_max_cnts(FVERTEX_OBJ 'src, FVERTEX_OBJ 'dst) { FVE

max_quad_cnt   < src->max_quad_cnt; dst->max_tri_cnt   < src->max_tri_cnt; dst->memlen   < src->memlen;] /*---------

d ----------------'/ void FVO_copy_vars(FVERTEX_OBJ 'src, FVERTEX_OBJ 'ds)] {'* no more copy_storm '/ FVO_copy_flags(src, dst);

EDWARD FELLA / LOS ANGELES

140 TO 169

Since the early seventies, Edward Fella has filled over fifty sketchbooks with his illustrations, collages, decorative types, ballpoint and color pencil drawings, and polaroid photographs. His work has been internationally honored and is represented in numerous publications. He teaches at the California Institute of Art in Los Angeles.

AMER-ARCANA. A JOURNEY FROM THE EAST COAST TO THE WEST COAST OF HIS AMERICAN MINDLAND. THIS IS A NARRATIVE SELECTION FROM A VAST CONTINENT COLLECTED DRAWINGS AND POLAROID PHOTOS OF HIS MAKING AND TAKING.

Seit den frühen siebziger Jahren füllt Edward Fella über fünfzig Skizzenbücher mit Illustrationen, Collagen, dekorativen Schriften, Kugelschreiber- und Buntstiftzeichnungen sowie Polaroid Fotografien. Seine Arbeit wurde international ausgezeichnet und in zahlreichen Publikationen vorgestellt. Er unterrichtet am California Institute of Arts in Los Angeles.

AMER-ARCANA. EINE REISE VON DER OST- ZUR WESTKÜSTE SEINER AMERIKANISCHEN GEDANKEN-LANDSCHAFT. EINE ERZÄHLERISCHE AUSWAHL AUS EINEM GEWALTIGEN KONTINENT SEINER GESAMMELTEN ZEICHNUNGEN UND POLAROIDS.

Evening
WALKERS

COME Stroll,

TWO for ONE,

DOWN-
WHILE THE

FISH DRY ON HIGH
STREETS
EDDUZ
WISE

A COUPLE Told
HANDED OVER FIST-
AND
WHILE THE
FISH FLY ON FRESH
SHEETS

A PAIR Hold
AND
CROSSED STAR BLISSED

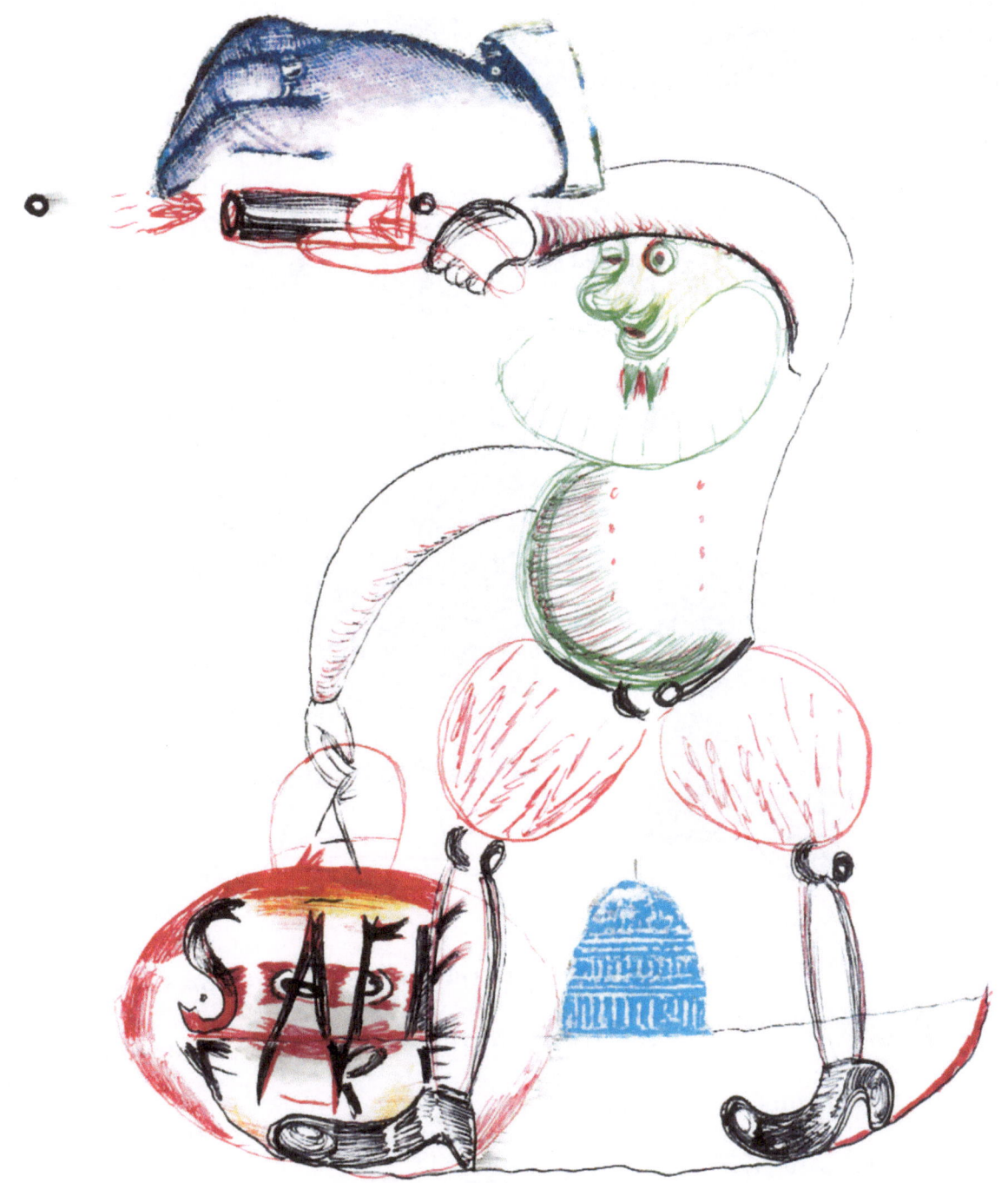

SEMIOSIS IN THE POSTMODERN AGE PEEL THE PARADOX OFFISH FROM THE MARGIN

IN EARLY MODERN PLAIN OL' HISTORY OF THE DESIRING FLIGHT TO THE OTHER

INTERPRETATION AGAINST ARGUMENTS OF WISSENSCHAFTSLEHRE METHODS IN

SOCIETY AND CIVIL INFORMATION AND THE ORIGIN OF THE AVERROISTS PHENOMENOLOGY

OF THE WORLD OF WISDOM IN THE NOCTURNAL STRANDS OF SYSTEM

Pry-out haunts
& RUMBLES

The Text: It's ONE o'clock in the afternoon this After the noon Meal meant to challenge change from EMPTY to FULL THE SECOND TIME TODAY around 1?, after FILLING up (at once) STILL holed up im after POPING off a few QUAILS im the bag shot WITH Game filled before SUPPER, after dinner; STOP, SHOOT ANY!
don't

ONE

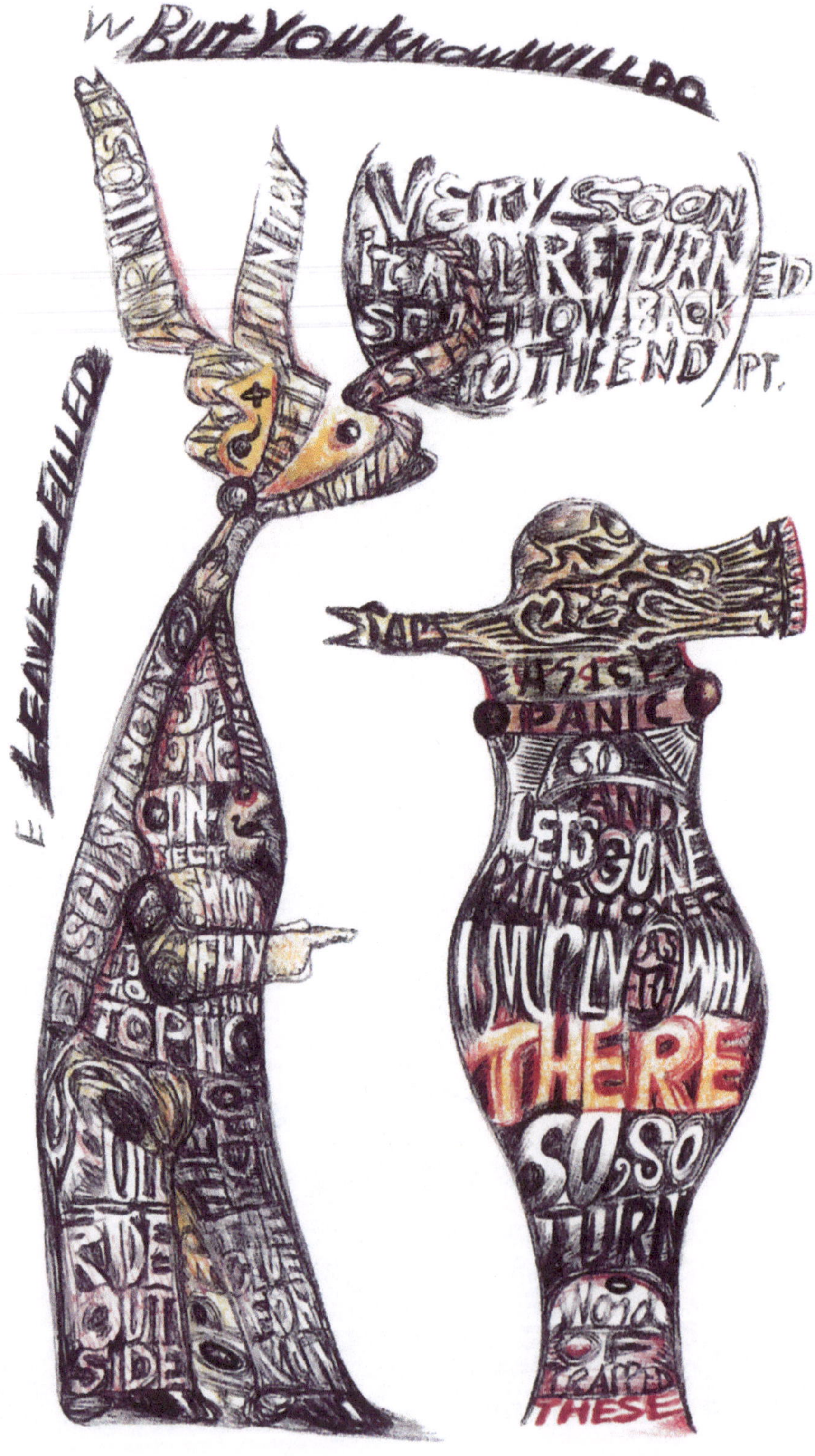

OUT WEST

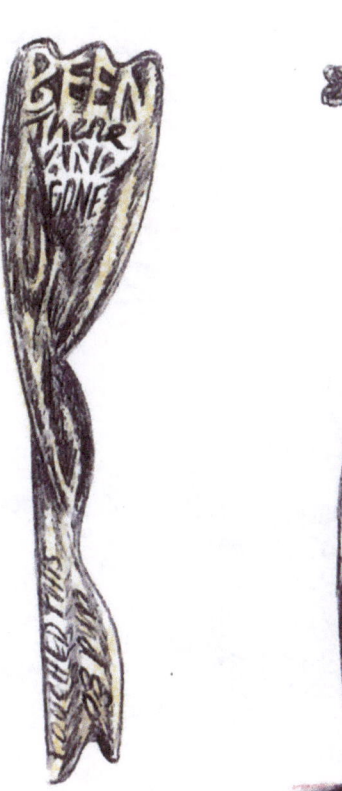

ROLF FEHLBAUM/VITRA

170 TO 189

The catastrophic fire on Vitra's premises in 1981 provided an impetus for renewal, both architectural and entrepreneurial. Rolf Fehlbaum is the businessman in a similar and special kind of way that Charles Eames was a designer.
(TRANSLATION ON PAGE 221)

Photography by Kay Michalak.

THIS CONTRIBUTION COMBINES ROLF FEHLBAUM'S IDEAS AND VIEWS WITH A PHOTOGRAPHIC PORTRAIT OF VITRA, A PLACE WHERE CREATIVE, COMMERCIAL, AND CULTURAL CONSIDERATIONS MEET.

Der verheerende Großbrand auf dem Firmengelände von Vitra im Jahr 1981 wurde zugleich zum Ausgangspunkt für eine architektonische und unternehmerische Neugestaltung des Unternehmens. Rolf Fehlbaum ist auf eine gewisse Art und Weise Unternehmer, wie Charles Eames Designer war.
(ÜBERSETZUNG AUF SEITE 221)

Fotografien von Kay Michalak.

DIESER BEITRAG VERBINDET IDEEN UND ANSICHTEN ROLF FEHLBAUMS MIT EINEM FOTOGRAFISCHEN PORTRAIT DES ORTES VITRA, AN DEM GESTALTERISCHE, KOMMERZIELLE UND KULTURELLE ÜBERLEGUNGEN AUFEINANDERTREFFEN.

Die Gemeinschaft funktioniert, weil die Menschen ungleich sind, und nicht etwa weil sie gleich sind.

attitude

Gestaltung der Wirtschaft Können Unternehmer und Manager das wirtschaftliche Geschehen überhaupt gestalten, oder sind sie nur mehr oder weniger geschickt operierende Figuren innerhalb einer zwingenden Logik, die ihnen, wenn sie erfolgreich werden oder bleiben wollen, eine Rolle vorschreibt.

Vitra Vitra steht nicht für einen Stil, sondern für eine Einstellung.

Zielgruppen Wir machen unsere Produkte nicht für durch Meinungsforschung herausdestillierte Zielgruppen. Ich glaube, man kann gerade dann gut für Zielgruppen arbeiten, wenn man an einen allgemeinen Nutzen denkt. Sobald man sich auf die Zielgruppe konzentriert, kommt es zu einer Zielgruppenanbiederung.

Image-Bildung/Marke Ich glaube, bei der Image-Bildung sind immer die Handlungen am wirksamsten, deren Einbindung in ein Unternehmensziel, zwar einsichtig ist, die gleichzeitig aber über das reine Nutzen- und Verantwortungsdenken hinausweisen. Eine Marke wird nicht dadurch gebaut, daß man einen Berater beauftragt, sich ein paar auffällige Ideen einfallen zu lassen. Sie entsteht, wenn man dem Alltagshandeln eine neue Dimension gibt. Es ist die Mischung von Selbstverständlichem und Überraschendem, die die Marke stärkt.

Design und Gesellschaft In großen gesellschaftlichen Umwälzungen hat das Design immer eine besondere Bedeutung. Wenn es stark ist, wird es Teil einer Reformbewegung. Design reduziert sich dann nicht einfach auf eine Disziplin, die im Marketing eingesetzt wird zur Optimierung der Verkäuflichkeit von Produkten.

»Religiöse« Unternehmen Meiner Meinung nach kommt das beste Design von Unternehmen, die ich aus Mangel an einer geeigneteren Bezeichnung »religiöse« Unternehmen nennen möchte. Das »religiöse« Unternehmen gleicht in vielerlei Hinsicht jedem anderen Unternehmen: Es muß Löhne auszahlen, es verfügt über einen bestimmten Endgewinn und es benötigt eine gute Unternehmensführung, um erfolgreich zu sein. Aber es verfolgt ein anderes Ziel. Das »religiöse« Unternehmen strebt nach einem Gewinn, der über den materiellen Profit hinausgeht. Dieses Unternehmen möchte etwas in Bezug auf die allgemeinen Vorstellungen einer Zeit oder einer Gesellschaft erreichen.

Erfolg Die Gefahr der »religiösen« Unternehmen besteht darin, daß sie zweifelhafte Menschen anziehen, verwirrte Menschen, die sagen: »Endlich ein Unternehmen, das nicht so materialistisch ist«. Wenn mich jemand mit diesen Worten anspräche, würde ich antworten: »Verzeihen Sie, wir sind sehr materialistisch, wir wollen sehr wohl Gewinne erzielen, wir wollen erfolgreich sein«.

Chancen und Pflichten Das designorientierte Unternehmen hat spezifische Chancen, Pflichten und Probleme. Zu den Pflichten gehört, daß man jedes Problem selbständig angeht. Natürlich lernt man von allem Bestehenden, aber das Ziel ist eine eigenständige neue Lösung. Aber das ist natürlich auch der Reiz: Permanente Aufbruchstimmung.

Unternehmensarchitektur Unser Architekturprogramm entstand nicht zum Zweck der Public Relation. Es wurde entwickelt um einen Ort zu schaffen, der aufregend und anders ist, gut für die Menschen, die hier arbeiten und gut für Besucher. Jedes Gebäude, das entsteht ist eine Chance, dem Unternehmen Identität zu geben und machtvoll nach innen und außen die Botschaft des Unternehmenswertes zu senden. Es gibt neben der Werbung keinen stärkeren Sender als das Gebäude.

Zusammenarbeit mit Designern Philippe Starck sagt: Ich bringe Ihnen dann und dann das Objekt und meint damit die Lösung. Bellini sagt: Ich will mich ganz leer von Vorstellungen machen. Entwickeln wir das Projekt zusammen in einem »Try and Error-Prozeß«. Jasper Morrison sucht die Normalität, das Verschwinden der Form. Frank Gehry sucht einen starken emotionalen Ausdruck. Wir arbeiten mit völlig unterschiedlichen Designern zusammen. Aber die Beziehungen sind immer Langzeitbeziehungen.

culture

Designprozeß Der Designprozeß ist dann erfolgreich, wenn ein Produkt entsteht, das mit Selbstverständlichkeit die wichtigsten Anforderungen erfüllt und eine Ausstrahlung hat, die Lust vermittelt. Zu dieser Designauffassung gehört auch die Einsicht, daß jedes Objekt, auch das banalste, und selbstverständlich umso mehr jeder Raum, jedes Gebäude ein Sender von Botschaften ist. In diesem Sinn vermittelt jedes Produkt eine Weltschau.

Design und Kunst Große Kunst und großes Design können die gleiche Wirkung hervorrufen, aber die Ausgangslage ist eine andere. Die schlimmste Zone ist die, die zwischen Design und Kunst liegt, wo die Objekte, die weder künstlerischen noch funktionellen Gesichtpunkten genügen, angesiedelt sind.

Charles Eames Eames hat sich sehr oft mit dem Design von Objekten befaßt, doch später interessierte er sich viel mehr für Fotografie, Film, Ausstellungen, Multimedia. Ich frage mich oft, ob Eames auch heutzutage noch Möbel entwerfen würde, und stelle mir vor, daß er sich wahrscheinlich für andere Dinge interessieren würde.

Herangehensweise Für mich war es nützlich, daß ich mich für viele Dinge interessiert habe, die mit Unternehmensführung nichts zu tun hatten. Alles, was zu gezielt ist, ist nur richtig für eine bestimmte Konstellation und Zeit. Eine offene, nicht unmittelbar in jeder Richtung zweckgebundene Identität ist vitaler, weil sie auch mit unterschiedlichen Situationen besser fertig wird und damit auch größere Entwicklungschancen bietet als etwas, das sehr geprägt oder festgelegt ist.

Eindeutigkeit Die Zeiten der Eindeutigkeit, auch wenn sie für viele die allerschönsten sind, weil sich Feind und Freund klar ausmachen lassen, sind heute vorbei. Wir erleben eine Phase, in der es eine ganze Reihe authentischer Antworten gibt. Wir wollen keinen Vitra-Stil und auch keine festgeschriebene Identität haben. Eindeutig und identifizierbar soll eine Werthaltung sein.

Fortführung des Projekts der Moderne Das Ziel war nicht, ein Einheitsmonument für Vitra zu schaffen, sondern einen Ort. Städte und Orte bestehen aus Unterschiedlichkeit und Spannungen – bis hin zum Konflikt zwischen sehr konträren Gebäuden. Was eint, ist eine gemeinsame Werthaltung. Dies ist für uns, und für alle Architekten, mit denen wir arbeiten, die Fortführung des Projekts der Moderne.

Das virtuelle Unternehmen Die Frage lautet: Was kommt Neues auf uns zu, und um wieviel flexibler müssen wir selber werden? Was heißt »Arbeit« überhaupt in Zukunft, was sind Unternehmen in 20 oder 30 Jahren? Was passiert, wenn »Firmen« oft nur mehr wechselnde Koalitionen von Lieferanten sind, die eng vernetzt sind, oft in fernen Ländern, die via Telekommunikation nahegerückt sind. Alles das ist ein Vorspiel zu einem globalen Spiel, in dem der Ort nicht mehr wichtig ist. Wie wir uns in so einer ortlosen Welt bewegen, und wieviel Flexibilität sie uns abfordert, das alles wird sich auch im Möbel niederschlagen.

Virtualisierung Die Virtualisierung, auch wenn sie sich heute noch nicht in ihrer Radikalität zeigt, hat unweigerlich eine Abwertung des Ortes zur Folge, eine Verflüchtigung des Ortes. Warum sich an einen Ort binden, wenn man nicht weiß, was in fünf Jahren ist. Diese Entwicklung zum Ephemeren ist der Architektur nicht förderlich.

Kulturelles Bewußtsein Man kann nicht MTV machen, ohne Teil dieser Kultur zu sein.

commerce

TOMATO / LONDON

190 TO 215

In a three-story building in London's Soho, members of the tomato collective weave together conversing and making and conversing again. Sometimes this process forms films, sometimes advertising, websites, CD-Roms, other forms of interactive media, they design books and buildings, or they write music or poetry.

THROUGH THE PROCESS OF PERSONAL NAVIGATION THE MAP IS CONTINUALLY REDRAWN, THE PROCESS OF PROCESS. THE WORLD EXPLAINS ITSELF. »A CONTINUOUS PROCESS ALTERED DAILY« ROBERT MORRIS

In einem dreistöckigen Loftgebäude in London's Soho wirken die Mitglieder von tomato zusammen, sich unterhaltend und schaffend und sich wieder unterhaltend. Manchmal entstehen aus diesem Prozeß Filme, manchmal Werbung, Webseiten, CD-Roms, andere interaktive Medien. Sie gestalten Bücher und Gebäude, schreiben Musik oder Gedichte.

DURCH DEN FORTLAUFENDEN PROZESS PERSÖNLICHER NAVIGATION WIRD DIE LANDKARTE STÄNDIG ERWEITERT, DER PROZESS DES PROZESSES. DIE WELT ERKLÄRT SICH SELBST. »EIN KONTINUIERLICHER PROZESS, DER SICH STÄNDIG ÄNDERT« ROBERT MORRIS

tomato

work in process
progress

wordless thing

ukiyo-e

the floating world;
the quantum present

inthisworldtogether

the world explains itself.
a 'continuous process altered daily'.

robert morris, the writings of robert morris, the mit press, 1993.

(and)

same

river

&

—————————————————————————

is

$$\frac{(\text{lost})}{\text{found}}$$

the map is inconclusive
since neither the internal nor external are static.
the map is inconclusive
since neither the form nor content are static.
the map is inconclusive
since neither the search nor journey are static.
the map is inconclusive
since neither the individual spirit nor the world are static.

in and out of sight
in and out of touch
in and out of mind
in and out of love
in and out of breath
in and out of line
in and out of bounds
in and out of space
in and out of time
in and out of
in and out
in   out

each speaks of the world as he sees it, but no one sees it in the same way. alain robbe-grillet, for a new novel, from realism to reality (1955 and 1963), p158.

PROCESS; IS

(WHEN YOU ARE NOT THINKING)

$$\frac{\text{WHAT GOES ON}}{\text{WHAT GOES ON}}$$

(WHEN YOU ARE THINKING)

THE END

BEGINNING

016 TO 041
P. SCOTT & LAURIE HAYCOCK MAKELA WITH PAUL SCHNEIDER

025 Schweigen ist eine der mächtigsten Übungen im Buddhismus. Ein Großteil unserer Gespräche besteht aus unbedeutendem Geplapper. Wer schweigt kann zuhören. Die Fehler anderer zu kritisieren erzeugt viel Leid. Wenn Du an wirklich Nichts und Niemandem mehr etwas auszusetzen hast, wirst Du ein außerordentlich glücklicher Mensch sein.

033 Durch all meine Ursachen und Wirkungen komme ich in diese Welt, in diesen Körper. Wo war ich vor diesem Körper? Und nach diesem Körper, wo werde ich sein? Die Menschen behandeln ihr Selbst wie einen Besitz. Aber das Selbst ist nur ein Traum, weil wir uns verändern. Die Essenz des Geistes ist leer. Wenn Du das erkennst, wird alles Phantasie – ein Trugbild, ein Hologramm, ein Traum. Du kannst Dich durch diese Leben bewegen, ohne den Tod zu fürchten. Du befindest Dich lediglich in einem Bus, an dem Bilder vorüberziehen. Wie alt bist Du? Du bist so alt wie der Urknall, Zeitverschwendung über vergangene Leben nachzudenken.

041 Die Sinne sind Instrumente und nicht befehlende Herrscher. Der Körper sagt: ich bin hungrig, ich bin müde, ich brauche Sex, ich will laufen, aber der Geist kann all das unterdrücken. Wenn Du Dich 21 Tage lang ohne Schlaf zurückziehst, sagt Dir Dein Geist, daß das nicht möglich ist. Im Buddhismus sagen wir »mit Hilfe harter Übung«. Die extreme Meditation versetzt Dich ins Hier und Jetzt.

096 TO 119
MAIRA & TIBOR KALMAN

100 »In den vergangenen Jahren wurde viel darüber geredet, daß die Welt »kleiner« wird – daß die Technologie, sei es das Düsenflugzeug, das Faxgerät oder der Satellit, die Unterschiede zwischen Kulturen und Menschen verwischt. Wir sind der Ansicht, daß dies nicht der Fall sein sollte. Die Botschaft dieser Zeitschrift lautet, daß Eure Kultur (wer immer Ihr seid) ebenso wichtig ist wie unsere Kultur (wer immer wir sind). Unserer Ansicht nach besteht der eigentliche Wert all dieser elektronischen Dinge, mit deren Hilfe andernfalls völlig voneinander isolierte Orte miteinander verbunden werden, darin, daß sie es uns ermöglichen, über den Tellerrand hinauszublicken und unsere Horizonte zu erweitern. Wir wollen wissen, was Ihr dort drüben treibt (wo immer Ihr seid) und wir sind uns ziemlich sicher, daß auch Ihr wissen wollt, was wir hier treiben (wo immer wir sind).«
(Auszug aus dem Editorial von »Colors« No. 1, It's a Baby, Herbst/Winter 1991)

120 TO 139
MICHAEL SAUP

123 Departure The installation R111 is a spatial ordering of various material, non-material, visual, acoustic, and tactile representations of an energy system.

125 Aggression Different virtual aggregate states manipulate the whole system, and the interaction of the users, as well as continual data transfer, supply it with energy. In the case of R111, this conversion of data and energy currents is supported by the algorithms of a computer program and its interaction with the information coming from its interfaces.

127 Disintegration The movements of the visitors and data that are fed in from the network guide the program, which is based on animation. A »sound floor« (floor panel guided by a motion-tracking system) functions as a user interface that records energy from movement. It represents the interface between the analogue and digital worlds of R111.

129 Abstraction A large »R« marks the hall as the heart of the installation. The room represents the »virtual world« of the system, while in another hall an aspect of it is shown as being something like »matter frozen in time.«

133 Fear In the neighboring rooms, references to additional material and non-material states dominate: desolate matter (pieces of stone and wall) next to electronic hardware as an interface with the World Wide Web, materialized sounds, or in line with the concept of Supreme Particles, accumulations of granulated matter.

135 Atom The theme of crossover between different artistic forms of expression is addressed in this installation through reference to a work which comes out of the beginnings of the art of animation: a film by Oskar Fischinger called »R–1« which the German artist produced in 1927. Fischinger, beside concise and »absolute« film animation, explored, above all, the interaction between sound and image in film. He is a historical stimulus for the installation by Supreme Particles. R111 is related to »R-1« and therefore also makes esoteric references »as with religious knowledge and/or that to which only initiates have access« to aspects of Fischeringer's work and also to the virtual system of Supreme Particles. Here, R111 can be seen as a reference to the number seven in the binary system, and so on.

137 Apathy At the same time, the installation reflects upon Francois Truffaut's film »Fahrenheit 451« from 1966 in more than its title (i.e., Netscape 451). It was a social-commentary and science fiction classic that dealt with the possibilities of subversive, individual resistance to power structures. Truffaut's film title (from the novel by Ray Bradbury) referred to the temperature at which books burn, and thus marked the transformation from one material state to another.

138 Molecule The multifaceted references and associations of R111 take the work beyond its interactive and visual presentation to a discussion about the openness of systems and the continuous interference from energy and matter (information).

170 TO 189
ROLF FEHLBAUM / VITRA

172 The community functions because people are not the same, and not because they are the same.

179 The chair No object is so closely connected to people as the chair. It has arms, legs, feet, and a back. It is a support for the human body; that is its physical task. It is, however, more than that: it represents the person. It says something about his/her status. And, of course, it says something about the epoch in which one uses it.

179 Design and society We can change society as little through new furniture as we can change sexuality through new beds. However, when change starts to emerge, we can express it and speed it up by means of architecture and design.

179 Life in the office I like the idea of having a library in the office that not only contains books that are essential for the work one does but which is also equipped with magazines and periodicals from other disciplines. And when one is tired, it is nice to be able to take a nap there. I want to have the feeling that I am not controlled by others. I need undefined rooms, »useless« rooms, which have no functional character.

179 The old office – The new office The problem with the old style of office design was the absence of any aesthetic pretensions and primitive hierarchical symbolism. The danger with the new offices is a different one: perfectly-styled workspaces are created that perfectly suit the business and its goals, but there is nowhere left for the individual to find a niche for him-/herself.

179 Design It would be a mistake to see design as the »aesthetizication« of the object. Design is the process of the integration of function, ergonomics, logistics of production, ecology, and the symbolism of a product – a complex mixture of considerations that, in part, are in conflict with each other.

179 Relevance I think we need a new form of consciousness of the problem of making products that are more »real«; otherwise, we just do »forms« and we become just stylists. I think sometimes styling is »ok.« It is not a terrible activity in itself; sometimes it is enough to give something a pleasant form. Of course it is not what I think is the basic task of design, because design is a method and a morale. And this is to do relevant things that matter. The core of the activity is to make products that are related to problems that have not been solved.

179 Anonymous design I am very interested in anonymous design and design from other parts of the world; other paths do exist. We have lost something of the sense of necessity, which has a great influence on the quality of design.

179 Real world For me personally, the designs which impress me the most come not from the Milan Exhibition but rather from the everyday world around us, and even more from the anonymous forms of structures and objects in daily use from Africa, India, and Indonesia.

179 Messages We are not doing anything revolutionary, but performing a service. Aware of the fact that every object is full of important messages, we can try to send decent ones, to contrast negative, authoritarian messages, and to enrich everyday experience.

179 Minimalism We always find the ideology that corresponds to the times and minimalism is an ideological response. It is a response to excess, but it is also a moralism that functions very well for our culture because it is only apparently austere. It is really a refined, demanding discipline, that can only function with the finest materials; it works on proportions and relations, which require quality and detailing. Costly materials and fine workmanship make such apparently simple products quite expensive.

181 Shaping the economy Can employers and managers actually shape the business world, or are they only more-or-less skillfully operating figures within a driving logic which prescribes a role for them to play if they want to be successful or, at the very least, just remain in the game?

181 Vitra does not have a style; it has an attitude.

181 Target groups We don't make our products for target groups distilled from market research findings. I believe that you can best work for target groups when you think of your own habits. As soon as you concentrate your efforts on the target group, it quickly turns into ingratiating yourself with the target group, groveling at its feet.

181 Creating the image/brand mark
I believe that when dealing with image creation, the most effective methods are always those whose integration into the aims of the business may be reasonable but that at the same time reach beyond the pure mentality of profit-and-responsibility. A trademark isn't created by asking an adviser to have a couple of interesting ideas. It happens when one gives the everyday a new dimension. It is the mixture of the obvious and the surprising that makes the trademark strong.

181 Design and society During times of great revolutionary changes in societies, design always has a particular significance. When it is strong, it is part of the reform movement. Design doesn't simply confine itself to a single discipline where it is employed in marketing or to improve the salability of products.

181 »Religious« companies I think that the best design comes from what I want to call for lack of a better word »religious« companies. The »religious« company is in many aspects like every other company; it has to pay salaries, has a bottom line, and has to be well run to succeed. But it has another desire. The »religious« company wants to be profitable for a reason beyond the profit. There is something this company wants to reach that relates to general ideas of a time or a society.

181 Success The danger of »religious« companies is that they attract phoney people, confused people who say »finally a company that is not so materialistic.« And if somebody approached me like this I would say »sorry, we are very materialistic, we want to be profitable, we want to be successful.«

181 Opportunity and onus The design-oriented enterprise has specific opportunities, onuses, and problems. The onus is on you to tackle every problem on your own. Of course, you learn from everything that exists, but the goal is an individual and new solution. On the other hand, that is of course also the attraction: permanent crisis mode.

181 Corporate architecture Our architectural programme was not designed for the purpose of public relations. It was undertaken to create a site which is exciting and different, good

for the people working here and good for visitors. Each building that is created provides an opportunity for giving the enterprise an identity, and to powerfully broadcast the message of the corporate values both internally and externally. Aside from advertising, there is no more powerful broadcaster of messages than the building.

181 Collaboration with designers Philippe Starck says, »I'll bring you the thing on such and such a date,« and what he means by »thing«is the solution. Bellini says, »I want to come to it free of any preconceptions. We'll develop the project together through trial and error.« Jasper Morrison seeks normality, the disappearance of form. Frank O. Gehry seeks strong emotional expression. We work with very different designers, but the relationships are always long-term.

183 Design process A design process is successful when a product is created which meets with the most important requirements in a self-evident way and radiates a sense of pleasure. This concept of design also includes the notion that every object, even the most banal, and obviously every room and every building, is a transmitter of a message. In this sense, every product conveys a particular view of the world.

183 Design and art Great art and great design can produce the same effect, but the starting point is different. The worst realm is the one that lies between design and art, where the objects which satisfy neither artistic nor functional requirements take up residence.

183 Charles Eames Eames often went back to designing objects, but later he was much more interested in photography, film, exhibitions, and multimedia. I often wonder if Eames would still design furniture today and imagine that he would probably be interested in other things.

183 Approaches It has been useful for me to have been interested in many things that have nothing to do with heading an enterprise. Everything that is very purposeful is only right for a certain constellation and time. An undefined identity, which is not immediately purpose bound in every direction, is more vital because it can cope better with a variety of situations and thereby offers greater opportunities for development than something that is very defined or determined.

183 Clarity The times of clarity, even though they are for many the best of all times because friend and foe declare themselves, are over today. We are experiencing a phase in which a whole row of authentic answers exist – we want no Vitra style and no predefined identity either. Values should be unequivocal and identifiable.

183 Continuation of the project of the modernism The aim was not to build a uniform monument to Vitra but rather a new place. Cities and places consist of variation and tension – right to the point of conflict between very opposing styles of building. Those things that unify are common values. This is, for us and for all architects with whom we work, the continuation of the project of the modernism.

183 The virtual enterprise The question is: What new things are coming and how much more flexible do we have to be? What will »work« mean in the future, what will business be in 20 or 30 years? What will happen when »firms« will often be merely ever-changing coalitions of suppliers that are closely networked but often in distant countries separated by great distances, and that have come closer together through advances in telecommunications? All this is a prelude to a global game in which location will no longer be important. How we get around in such a placeless world and how much flexibility it will demand of us will also be reflected in the world of furniture.

183 Virtualization Virtualization, even if it has not yet revealed itself in all its radical dimensions, will lead unquestionably to the devaluation of the place, a curse on the place. Why bind yourself to a place when no one knows what will happen in five years' time? This trend towards the ephemeral is not beneficial to architecture.

183 Cultural awarness You cannot do MTV without being a part of that culture.

016 TO 041
P. SCOTT & LAURIE HAYCOCK MAKELA
CRANBROOK

Laurie Haycock Makela graduated from the Rhode Island School of Design and earned her MFA in 1991 from the Cranbrook Academy of Arts.
She was design director at the renowned Walker Arts Center Minneapolis, and her exhibition catalogues for Spirit of Fluxus, Bruce Nauman and Willem de Kooning have earned her many design awards. For many years, Laurie taught at the California Institute of the Arts and the Otis Art Institute in Los Angeles.

Scott Makela was born in St. Paul, Minnesota and studied at the California Institute of the Arts and later at the Cranbrook Academy of Arts.
He produced music videos for Miles Davis, 10 000 Maniacs, Urge Overkill, and Michael Jackson.
To those, he added films and videos for Nike, MTV, Kodak, Lotus Software, and Propaganda Films as well as the title sequence for the feature film »The Game« and the recently released »Fight Club« by David Fincher and Jeffrey Plansker.
His recent works included a number of videos for MTV and a print and Internet campaign for Rossignol Ski and Snowboards.

The two jointly headed the 2D-faculty at Cranbrook and ran their own design studio »Words + Pictures for Business + Culture.« They gave lectures worldwide and their work has been pictured in many design publications. Alongside their design work, they produced their second music CD »Addictions + Meditations.« Their book »whereishere,« which was published in the autumn of 1998, deals with the theme of position and obsession in film, design, and photography.

Scott Makela died on May 7th, 1999, at the age of 39. Laurie Haycock Makela lives with their two children near Detroit.

Laurie Haycock Makela graduiert an der Rhode Island School of Design und absolviert 1991 ihr MFA an der Cranbrook Academy of Arts.
Sie wird Design Director des berühmten Walker Arts Center Minneapolis und ihre Ausstellungskataloge für Spirit of Fluxus, Bruce Nauman und Willem de Kooning erhalten zahlreiche Auszeichnungen. Mehrere Jahre unterrichtet Laurie Haycock Makela am California Institute of the Arts und dem Otis Art Institute in Los Angeles.

Scott Makela wird in St. Paul, Minnesota geboren und studiert am California Institute of the Arts und später an der Cranbrook Academy of Arts.
Er produziert Musikvideos für Miles Davis, 10 000 Maniacs, Urge Overkill und Michael Jackson.
Darüber hinaus entstehen Filme und Videos für Nike, MTV, Kodak, Lotus Software und Propaganda Films sowie die Titelsequenz für den Spielfilm »The Game« und »Fight Club« von David Fincher und Jeffrey Plansker. Zu seinen letzten Arbeiten gehören mehrere Videos für MTV und eine Print und Internet Kampagne für Rossignol Ski und Snowboards.

Gemeinsam leiten sie den 2-D Bereich in Cranbrook und betreiben ihr eigenes Designstudio »Words + Pictures for Business + Culture«. Weltweit halten sie Vorträge und ihre Arbeiten werden in zahlreichen Publikationen vorgestellt. Neben ihrer Designarbeit produzieren sie ihre zweite Musik-CD »Addictions + Meditations«. Ihr Buch »whereishere«, das im Herbst 1998 erschien beschäftigt sich mit dem Thema: Position und Obsession in Film, Design und Fotografie.

Scott Makela starb am 7. Mai 1999 im Alter von 39 Jahren. Laurie Haycock Makela lebt mit ihren gemeinsamen zwei Kindern in der Nähe von Detroit.

042 TO 069
PETER REA LONDON

Peter Rea was born in Dublin, Eire in 1938, and has lived in London most of his life. His time is divided equally between design and teaching. He studied at the Wimbledon School of Art, the London College of Printing (LCP), and the Royal College of Art. In 1971/72 Peter Rea was a visiting assistent professor at PCA, University of the Arts, Philadelphia: a major catalyst for internationalists. Between 1972 and 1980 he was head of the Advanced Typography LCP.
From 1980 to 1984 head of the School of Graphic Design, Leicester, where his graduates included Sean Perkins from North. From 1988 to 1991 he was head of the Ravensbourne College, London.

His design work includes graphics, installations and exhibitions for the Institute of Contemporary Arts in London, the Photographers Gallery London, and for professional clients.

As visiting professor at the Hochschule für Künste in Bremen, he developed the New Intermedia Centre, which lies somewhere between the traditional areas of film, music, fashion, and graphic design. In 1998 he created, together with Dorthe Meinhardt, Sven Voelker, and Thomas Weiling, the first profile intermedia conference in Bremen.
Besides working on the European and American continents, he has been professor of art and design at the Notre Dame University, Beirut, for the last 5 years.

Peter Rea is the inspirational source of this book and initiator of many projects including profile intermedia 2 conference in December 1999.
Peter Rea lives and works in London, Beirut, and Bremen.

Peter Rea wird 1938 in Dublin, Irland geboren und verbringt einen Großteil seines Lebens in London, zu gleichen Teilen mit Design und dem Lehren. Er studiert an der Wimbledon School of Art, dem London College of Printing (LCP) und dem Royal College of Art. 1971/72 ist Peter Rea Gastprofessor am PCA, University of the Arts, Philadelphia: ein Treffpunkt für Menschen aus der ganzen Welt. Zwischen 1972 und 1980 leitet er das Advanced Typography am LCP. Von 1980 bis 1984 ist er Leiter der School of Graphic Design, Leicester, wo Sean Perkins von NORTH zu seinen Studenten gehört. 1988 bis 1991 ist er Schulleiter des Ravensbourne College in London.

Seine gestalterische Arbeit umfaßt Grafik Design, Installationen und Ausstellungen für das Institute of Contemporary Arts in London, die Photographers Gallery London und andere Kunden.

Als Gastprofessor an der Hochschule für Künste Bremen entwickelt er das New Intermedia Centre, das zwischen den traditionellen Bereichen Film, Musik, Mode und Grafik Design liegt. 1998 initiiert er gemeinsam mit Dorthe Meinhardt, Sven Voelker und Thomas Weiling die erste profile intermedia Konferenz in Bremen.
Neben seiner Arbeit auf dem europäischen und amerikanischen Kontinent, ist er seit 5 Jahren Professor für Kunst und Design an der Notre Dame University, Beirut.

Peter Rea ist die Inspirationsquelle dieses Buches und Initiator vieler Projekte, darunter auch die profile intermedia 2 Konferenz im Dezember 1999. Peter Rea lebt und arbeitet in London, Beirut und Bremen.

070 TO 095
NORTH LONDON

North was founded in 1995 by Simon Browning and Sean Perkins. They first met in 1987 and have worked together at various graphic design and brand companies (Peter Leonard Associates, Cartlidge Levene). At Wolff Olins in 1989 Sean Perkins created the design for and launched »First Direct,« an award winning radical departure from high street banking, and in 1995 was responsible for the concept and design of the critically acclaimed book »Experience.«

Since its foundation the design team has expanded and completed design programs for a range of national and international clients. These include the RAC, Andersen Consulting, Selfridges & Co, Syn Productions Co (Tokyo), Ikepod Watch Co AG, The Mill, Hugo Boss, Photographers Gallery, Serpentine Gallery (London) and others.

North's complete and radical redesign of the RAC (Royal Automobile Club), one of Britain's great institutions, in 1997/98 created an identity that in a few years has been established as a memorable part of Britain's urban landscape. North excels in a range of design disciplines and is frequently invited to lecture and exhibit at design conferences throughout Europe, America, and Japan.

North wird 1995 von Simon Browning und Sean Perkins gegründet. Sie treffen sich erstmals 1987 und arbeiteten in verschiedenen Grafik Design- und Brand-Unternehmen zusammen (Peter Leonard Associates, Cartlidge Levene). 1989 bei Wolff Olins übernimmt Sean Perkins das Design und die Einführung von »First Direct«, ein preisgekrönter, radikaler Abschied vom High Street Banking. 1995 ist er verantwortlich für Konzept und Design des von den Kritikern gefeierten Buches »Experience«.

Seit seiner Gründung hat sich das Design-Team vergrößert und es werden unterschiedliche Design-Programme für eine Vielzahl von nationalen und internationalen Kunden entwickelt.
Dazu zählen unter anderem der RAC, Andersen Consulting, Selfridges & Co, Syn Productions co (Tokyo), Ikepod Watch Co AG, The Mill, Hugo Boss, Photographers Gallery, Serpentine Gallery (London) und andere.

1997/98 schafft North ein vollständig und radikal neues Design des RAC (Royal Automobile Club), eine der großen Institutionen Großbritanniens, eine Corporate Identity, die sich in nur wenigen Jahren als einprägsamer Teil der Landschaft Großbritanniens etabliert.

North ist in einer Vielzahl von Design-Bereichen erfolgreich und wird regelmäßig zu Vorträgen und Ausstellungen auf Design-Konferenzen in Europa, Amerika und Asien eingeladen.

096 TO 119
MAIRA & TIBOR KALMAN
NEW YORK

In the mid-fifties, Tibor Kalman came from Hungary and Maira from Israel with their families to the United States. They met in 1968 at New York University and became a couple in private and professionally.

Maira finished her studies in literature by starting to paint her thoughts instead of writing them down. Since then she has published ten successful children's books, among them a series about Max Stravinsky, the poet dog who travels around the world. Among others, she was an illustrator for the New Yorker and New York Times and designed fabrics for the fashion designer Isaac Mizrahi. Her work was admitted into the permanent collection of the Children's Museum of Manhattan.

Tibor worked in a small book store during his studies; due to its owners' abilities it became the successful book enterprise Barnes & Noble and Tibor became its marketing and corporate design director. In 1979, he founded his own office and called it M&Co, the »M« representing Maira. During the eighties, Tibor became the »bad boy« of the scene andone of the most successful personalities in graphic design.

In 1991, Tibor received the commission to publish a magazine by Benetton. »Colors« was the result, and after the first five issues the Kalmans emigrated to Italy. After having worked on »Colors« for five years, Tibor was told that he had cancer and they both returned to New York. During this time the book »Chairman« about Rolf Fehlbaum was written and designed.

On May 2nd, 1999, Tibor Kalman died at the age of fifty. Maira Kalman lives in New York with their two children.

Mitte der Fünfziger Jahre kommen Tibor Kalman aus Ungarn und Maira aus Israel mit ihren Familien in die USA.

An der New York University begegnen sich die beiden 1968 zum ersten Mal und werden privat und beruflich zu einem Paar.

Ihr Literaturstudium beendet Maira, indem sie anfängt ihre Gedanken zu malen, statt sie aufzuschreiben. Seitdem veröffentlicht sie zehn erfolgreiche Kinderbücher, darunter eine Serie über Max Stravinsky, einem Hund, der dichtet und um die Welt reist. Sie illustriert unter anderem für den New Yorker und die New York Times und entwirft Stoffe für den Modedesigner Isaac Mizrahi. Arbeiten von ihr werden in die ständige Sammlung des Children's Museum of Manhattan aufgenommen.

Tibor arbeitet neben seinem Studium in einem kleinen Buchladen, der durch die Geschicke seines Besitzers zum erfolgreichen Buchunter-nehmen Barnes & Noble und Tibor zu dessen Marketing- und Corporate-Design Director wird. 1979 gründet er sein eigenes Büro und nennt es M&Co, wobei das »M« für Maira steht. Im Verlauf der Achtziger Jahre wird Tibor zum »Bad Boy« in der Szene und zu einem der erfolgreichsten Persönlichkeiten im Grafik Design. 1991 erhält er von Benetton den Auftrag ein

Magazin herauszubringen. Es entsteht »Colors«, und nach den ersten fünf Ausgabe wandern die Kalmans nach Italien aus. Nach fünf Jahren Arbeit an »Colors« erfährt Tibor, daß er an Krebs erkrankt ist, woraufhin die beiden nach New York zurückkehren. In dieser Zeit entsteht unter anderem das Buch »Chairman« über Rolf Fehlbaum.

Am 2. Mai 1999 stirbt Tibor Kalman im Alter von 50 Jahren. Maira Kalman lebt mit ihren beiden Kindern in New York.

120 TO 139
MICHAEL SAUP
FRANKFURT

Michael Saup was born in 1961 in Hechingen/ Hohenzollern. After studying music in California and information science in Furtwangen, he studied visual communication between 1984 and 1992 at the Hochschule für Gestaltung in Offenbach.

While carrying out various teaching contracts in Munich, Karlsruhe, Bremen, and Offenbach, in 1992 he founded the group Supreme Particles in Frankfurt and San Francisco with Anna Saup and Gideon May. From 1990 to 1994 he collaborated with Peter Weibel at the Institute for New Media in Frankfurt am Main.

His interactive installations are based on the interaction between observer, machine, and space. In »Plasma/Architexture« from 1994, for example, the observer manipulates the sounds and images produced by the installation with his or her movements.

Michael Saup is professor of Media Arts at the Hochschule für Gestaltung in Karlsruhe. He lives and works in Frankfurt am Main.

Michael Saup wird 1961 in Hechingen/Hohenzollern geboren. Nach dem Studium der Musik in Kalifornien und der Informatik in Furtwangen, studiert er zwischen 1984 und 1992 an der Hochschule für Gestaltung in Offenbach Visuelle Kommunikation.

Parallel zu seinen Lehraufträgen in München, Karlsruhe, Bremen und Offenbach gründet er 1992 gemeinsam mit Anna Saup und Gideon May die Gruppe Supreme Particles. Von 1990 bis 1994 arbeitet er mit Peter Weibel am Institut für Neue Medien in Frankfurt am Main.

Seine interaktiven Installationen basieren auf der Interaktion zwischen Betrachter, Maschine und Raum. In »Plasma/Architexture« von 1994 manipuliert der Betrachter zum Beispiel mit seinen Bewegungen Klang und Bild der Installation.

Michael Saup ist Professor für Medienkunst an der Hochschule für Gestaltung Karlsruhe. Er lebt und arbeitet in Frankfurt/Main.

140 TO 169
EDWARD FELLA
LOS ANGELES

Edward Fella, the son of German immigrants, was born in Detroit in 1938. After studying commercial art at the Technical High School in Detroit, he worked for 30 years as a graphic designer and illustrator in Detroit.

While creating many commercial works, which he valued for the experience and remuneration they gave him, he also continuously experimented during this time.

In accordance with the Autoworkers' Union motto »thirty and out,« in the middle of the eighties he decided to give up professional work and to study for a master's degree for two years at the

Cranbrook Academy of Arts. In 1987 he was appointed to the position of professor at the famous California Institute of the Arts where he still teaches today and devotes himself full-time to his own work.

Since the early seventies he has filled over fifty sketch books with his illustrations, collages, and ballpoint and color-pencil drawings; a project of reworking the subject and techniques of his former commercial practice through a free and completely idiosyncratic exploration.
He has also taken over 3000 polaroid photographs of fragments of signs, lettering, and pictorial emphemera in the vernacular landscape found throughout America.

Ed Fella has received international recognition for his work and has been frequently invited to lecture at international conferences and schools. He lives and works in Los Angeles.

Edward Fella wird 1938 als Sohn deutscher Einwanderer in Detroit geboren. Nach seinem Design-Studium an der Technical Highschool in Detroit arbeitet er 30 Jahre als Illustrator, Fotograf und Typograf in Detroits Kraftfahrzeug Industrie.

Während er viele kommerzielle Arbeiten ausführt, die er aufgrund der durch sie gesammelten Erfahrung und auch erzielten Bezahlung schätzt, erstellt er in dieser Zeit auch fortwährend experimentelle Arbeiten.

Im Einklang mit dem Motto der Autoworkers Union, »thirty and out«, beschließt er Mitte der Achtziger Jahre, das Berufsleben aufzugeben und sich zwei Jahre lang dem Studium für ein Masters Degree an der Cranbrook Academy of Arts zu widmen. 1987 wird er als Professor an das renommierte California Institute of the Arts berufen, wo er bis heute unterrichtet und sich fortwährend mit seinen eigenen Arbeiten beschäftigt.

Seit den Siebziger Jahren füllt er über fünfzig Skizzenbücher mit seinen Illustrationen, Collagen, Kugelschreiber- und Buntstiftzeichnungen. Ein Projekt, in dem das Thema und die Techniken seiner früheren, kommerziellen Praxis durch eine freie und idiosynkratische Erforschung überarbeitet wurden.

Ed Fella erhält für seine Arbeit internationale Anerkennung und wird zu Vorträgen auf internationalen Konferenzen und Schulen eingeladen. Er lebt und arbeitet in Los Angeles.

170 TO 189
ROLF FEHLBAUM / VITRA

Rolf Fehlbaum was born in Basel in 1941. His parents Willi and Erika Fehlbaum, founded the firm Vitra in 1950 in Weil am Rhein. In 1957 they began to manufacture furniture designs by Charles & Ray Eames and George Nelson under license to Herman Miller, USA, for the European market.

Rolf Fehlbaum graduated with a degree in sociology and wrote a thesis for his doctorate on »The Utopian Socialism of St. Simon.« Following a period of very diverse activities – for example, as founder of an art publishing house, as a director in a film production company, and as an assistant for continuing training in architecture in Munich – he took over the management of Vitra.

After a serious fire at the factory in 1981, in consultation with architects like Frank O. Gehry, Nicholas Grimshaw, Tadao Ando, and Zaha M. Hadid, he embarked on an architectural renewal and, consequently, a business reappraisal of Vitra. Rolf Fehlbaum and Vitra have received many awards, among them the »Design Preis Schweiz« (Swiss Design Award), the »Design Award« from Industrie Forum Design, Hanover and the »Bundespreis für Förderer.«

In 1989, the Vitra Design Museum in Weil am Rhein was created, and five years later, Vitra's new central administrative building was opened in Birsfelden near Basel. Rolf Fehlbaum lives and works in Basel.

Rolf Fehlbaum wird 1941 in Basel geboren. Seine Eltern Willi und Erika Fehlbaum gründen 1950 das Unternehmen Vitra in Weil am Rhein. Ab 1957 beginnt man Möbelentwürfe von Charles und Ray Eames und George Nelson in Lizenzproduktion von Herman Miller/USA für den europäischen Markt herzustellen.

Rolf Fehlbaum absolviert das Studium der Sozialwissenschaften und promoviert über den »utopischen Sozialismus Saint-Simons«. Nach sehr unterschiedlichen Tätigkeiten als Gründer eines Kunstverlags, Redakteur bei einer Filmproduktionsfirma und als Referent für Architektur-Weiterbildung in München, übernimmt er 1977 die Leitung von Vitra.

Nach einem Großbrand auf dem Firmengelände im Jahr 1981 beginnt er gemeinsam mit Architekten wie Frank O. Gehry, Nicholas Grimshaw, Tadao Ando und Zaha M. Hadid die architektonische, und damit die unternehmerische Neugestaltung von Vitra. Rolf Fehlbaum und Vitra werden zahlreiche Auszeichnungen verliehen, darunter auch der »Design Preis Schweiz«, der »Design Award« des Industrie Forum Design Hannover und der »Bundespreis für Förderer«.

1989 entsteht das Vitra Design Museum in Weil am Rhein, fünf Jahre später wird das zentrale Verwaltungsgebäude von Vitra in Birsfelden bei Basel eröffnet. Rolf Fehlbaum lebt und arbeitet in Basel.

190 TO 215
TOMATO LONDON

tomato was founded in 1991, in London, by Steve Baker, Dirk van Dooren, Karl Hyde, Rick Smith, Simon Taylor, John Warwicker, and Graham Wood. After only a short time, it has developed into one of the more decisive influences in European and international graphic design.

John Warwicker, who is working at the moment on an architectural project in Melbourne, Australia, says of tomato's work, »I have never understood the necessity of differentiating between commercial and personal work, it's just work: either I, tomato or a third party form a space for the work to happen.«

Tomato's work concerns itself with processes and experiences. Through the combining of collective and personal forms of expression, products are created in the most varied of contexts.
For this book, John Warwicker has shaped his thoughts on the process, in a form of concrete poetry. All the members of tomato live and work in London.

tomato wird 1991 von Steve Baker, Dirk van Dooren, Karl Hyde, Rick Smith, Simon Taylor, John Warwicker und Graham Wood in London gegründet. In kurzer Zeit entwickelt sich die Gruppe zu einem der entscheidenen Einflüße für das europäische und internationale Grafik Design.

John Warwicker, der zur Zeit an einem Architektur Projekt in Melbourne, Australien arbeitet, meint zur Arbeit von tomato: »Ich habe die Notwendigkeit zur Unterscheidung zwischen kommerzieller und freier Arbeit nie wirklich verstanden, es ist eben nur Arbeit. Ich, tomato oder eine dritte Person schafft den Raum, in der diese Arbeit stattfindet.«

Die Arbeit von tomato beschäftigt sich mit Prozessen und Erlebnissen. Durch die Verbindung von gemeinsamen und persönlichen Ausdrucksformen entstehen Produkte in den unterschiedlichsten Zusammenhängen.

Für dieses Buch gestaltete John Warwicker seine Gedanken dazu in einer Form von konkreter Poesie. Alle Mitglieder von tomato leben und arbeiten in London.

PROPELLERS

Early in 1999 a part of the organizers of the first profile intermedia conference in Bremen founded the art- and design-network Propellers in cooperation with members of the Bremen-based design group GfG – Gruppe für Gestaltung.

The potential within the idea of intermedia offers a platform for new projects and for collaboration with people from very different creative disciplines.
You can find more information on the people behind Propellers and their projects on: www.propellers.org or contact Propellers at mail@propellers.org.

Im Frühjahr 1999 gründeten ein Teil der Organisatoren der ersten profile intermedia Konferenz, gemeinsam mit Mitgliedern der Bremer Designgruppe GfG (Gruppe für Gestaltung) das Design- und Kunst-Network Propellers.

Das Potential der Ideen, die hinter dem Wort Intermedia stehen, bietet der Gruppe eine Plattform für neuartige Projekte und für eine Zusammenarbeit mit Gestaltern aus den unterschiedlichsten Bereichen.
Mehr Informationen zu den Menschen hinter Propellers und den aktuellen Projekten befinden sich auf www.propellers.org,
Kontakt zu Propellers über: mail@propellers.org.

DORTHE MEINHARDT
BREMEN

Dorthe Meinhardt was born in Lemgo in 1972. She began her study in the field of visual communication at the Fachhochschule in Würzburg. After a semester studying at the Ecole de Beaux Arts in Toulouse, France, she transferred to the Hochschule für Künste in Bremen in 1995. Besides pursuing her course of study, she worked for the Bremen-based design studio jung und pfeffer and later for the GfG – Gruppe für Gestaltung.

In 1998 she took part in the organization and shaping of the first profile intermedia conference. Following the success of the event, she, along with Sven Voelker and members of the GfG – Gruppe für Gestaltung, founded the group called Propellers. Apart from this book, an additional project undertaken by the art and design group is the »Propellers Internet Art Gallery« (at http://www.propellers.org).
Dorthe Meinhardt lives and works in Bremen.

Dorthe Meinhardt wird 1972 in Lemgo geboren. Sie beginnt ihr Studium im Bereich Visuelle Kommunikation an der Fachhochschule Würzburg. Nach einem Auslandssemester an der Ecole des Beaux Arts in Toulouse, Frankreich wechselt sie 1995 an die Hochschule für Künste Bremen. Neben dem Studium arbeitet sie für das Bremer Designbüro jung und pfeffer und später für die GfG – Gruppe für Gestaltung.

1998 beteiligt sie sich an der Organisation und Gestaltung der ersten profile intermedia Konferenz. Nach dem erfolgreichen Abschluß der Veranstaltung, gründet sie gemeinsam mit Sven Voelker und Mitgliedern der »Gruppe für Gestaltung« die Gruppe Propellers. Neben diesem Buch ist die »Propellers Internet Art Gallery« ein weiteres Projekt der Design- und Kunstgruppe. (http://www.propellers.org)
Dorthe Meinhardt lebt und arbeitet in Bremen.

SVEN VOELKER
BERLIN

Sven Voelker was born in Coesfeld in 1974. From 1994 to 1998 he studied graphic design at the Hochschule für Künste in Bremen. There, he interested himself in the ideas of intermedia and completed his diploma with a presentation on »flexibility and change.«

After having worked for the design studio Imagination in London in 1997, he returned to Bremen to organize, along with Dorthe Meinhardt, Peter Rea, and Thomas Weiling, the profile intermedia conference. In December 1998 artists working in the most varied creative disciplines met together to discuss media crossover. With 1200 attending, profile intermedia 98 was one of the most successful events of its kind. Together with Dorthe Meinhardt, he has edited and designed this book in a one-year process.

Besides working as a freelance designer for various design studios and on his own projects, he is studying for a Master of Arts degree in London. Sven Voelker lives and works in Berlin.

Sven Voelker wird 1974 in Coesfeld geboren. Von 1994 bis 1998 studiert er an der Hochschule für Künste in Bremen Grafik Design. Dort beschäftigte er sich mit den Ideen von Intermedia und diplomiert mit einer Arbeit über »flexibility and change«.

Nachdem er 1997 für das Designbüro Imagination in London arbeitet, kehrt er nach Bremen zurück, um gemeinsam mit Dorthe Meinhardt, Peter Rea und Thomas Weiling die profile intermedia Konferenz zu organisieren. Im Dezember 1998 treffen Gestalter aus den verschiedensten Bereichen zusammen, um über Medien Crossover zu diskutieren. Mit 1200 Besuchern gehört die profile intermedia 98 zu den erfolgreichsten Veranstaltungen ihrer Art.

Gemeinsam mit Dorthe Meinhardt entwickelte und gestaltete er dieses Buch in einem Prozess, der sich über ein Jahr erstreckte.

Neben seiner Tätigkeit als freier Gestalter für verschiedene Designbüros und seiner Arbeit an eigenen Projekten absolviert er zur Zeit sein Master of Art in London. Sven Voelker lebt und arbeitet in Berlin.

016 TO 041   **P. SCOTT & LAURIE HAYCOCK**
MAKELA WITH PAUL SCHNEIDER
CONCEPT + DESIGN
Laurie Haycock Makela,
Paul Schneider

Faith in Action, God is close,
and Vertigo is fun created for
Rossignol Ski and Snowboards
by P. Scott Makela in April 1999

VIDEO PHOTOGRAPHY
David Crabb, Kurt Miller,
Sevrin Henderson

042 TO 069   **PETER REA**
CONCEPT +TEXT
Peter Rea

DESIGN
Peter Rea with special
thanks for assistance from
Florian Pfeffer

PHOTOGRAPHY
Jacky Chapman, Janine Wiedel
with additional thanks to
Stuart Brown

070 TO 095   **NORTH**
CONCEPT + DESIGN
North

PHOTOGRAPHY (except 086-088)
Amber Rowlands

096 TO 119   **MAIRA & TIBOR KALMAN**
098 TO 099   ILLUSTRATION
Maira Kalman

100 TO 101   Colors 1: It's a Baby
TEXT: excerpt from the editorial
IMAGE: Detail of the cover
Editorial Director: Oliviero Toscani
Editor-In-Chief: Tibor Kalman
Design: Emily Oberman

102 TO 103   Colors 8: Religion
IMAGE: Details of page 62-63
Editorial Director: Oliviero Toscani
Editor-In-Chief: Tibor Kalman
Art Director: Scott Stowell

´104 TO 105   Colors 4: Race
IMAGE: Page 30-31
Editorial Director: Oliviero Toscani
Editor-In-Chief: Tibor Kalman
Design: Paul Ritter

107   Colors 2: Immigration
IMAGE: Detail of the cover
Editorial Director: Oliviero Toscani
Editor-In-Chief: Tibor Kalman
Design: Gary Koepke

108 TO 109   Colors 5: Eat the Street
IMAGE: Part of page 46-47
Editorial Director: Oliviero Toscani
Editor-In-Chief: Tibor Kalman
Design: Paul Ritter

110 TO 111   Colors 5: Eat the Street
IMAGE: Part of page 48-49
Editorial Director: Oliviero Toscani
Editor-In-Chief: Tibor Kalman
Design: Paul Ritter

112 TO 113   Colors 6: Ecology Now
IMAGE: Part of page 78-79
Editorial Director: Oliviero Toscani
Editor-In-Chief: Tibor Kalman
Design: Scott Stowell

114   Colors 6: Ecology Now
IMAGE: Part of page 22
Editorial Director: Oliviero Toscani
Editor-In-Chief: Tibor Kalman
Design: Scott Stowell

115   Colors 1: It's a Baby
IMAGE: Detail of page 18
Editorial Director: Oliviero Toscani
Editor-In-Chief: Tibor Kalman
Design: Emily Oberman

116 TO 117   Colors 7: AIDS Special
IMAGE: Detail of page 104-105
Editorial Director: Oliviero Toscani
Editor-In-Chief: Tibor Kalman
Design: Scott Stowell

118 TO 119   Colors 12: Heaven
IMAGES: Detail of page 2-3
Editorial Director: Oliviero Toscani
Editor-In-Chief: Tibor Kalman
Art Director: Mark Porter

120 TO 139   **MICHAEL SAUP**
CONCEPT
Michael Saup, Supreme Particles

DESIGN
Thomas Weiling
assisted by Michael Saup

PHOTOGRAPHY
Karl Dittrich, Eberhard Hoch,
Thomas Kersten, Anne Niemetz,
Michael Saup, Frank Schuberth,
Thomas Weiling, Wilfried Wirth,
Wilhelm Lehmbruck Museum
Duisburg

TEXT
Katharina Gsöllpointner

140 TO 169   **EDWARD FELLA**
CONCEPT + DESIGN
Edward Fella

170 TO 189   **ROLF FEHLBAUM**
TEXT
Rolf Fehlbaum

PHOTOGRAPHY
Kay Michalak

190 TO 215   **TOMATO**
CONCEPT + DESIGN
John Warwicker, tomato

001 TO 015   **PROPELLERS**
216 TO 240   CONCEPT + DESIGN
Dorthe Meinhardt, Sven Voelker,
Propellers

IMPRESSUM 233

EDITED AND DESIGNED

by Dorthe Meinhardt and Sven Voelker
at Propellers from an idea developed
with Peter Rea and Thomas Weiling.

PROPELLERS

Am Dobben 147, 28203 Bremen, Germany
http://www.propellers.org
mail@propellers.org

BEYOND THE BORDERS

is published as Volume 8 within the essay
series »Design im Kontext«
edited by Dieter Kretschmann for the
Rat für Formgebung/German Design Council.

MANY THANKS TO

GfG – Gruppe für Gestaltung, Hanke Homburg,
Thomas Kleiner, Meaghan Kombol at M&Co,
Michaela Kopp at Papier Union, Frank Minkwitz
at Headline, and Carlos Mustienes at
Colors Magazine.

AUTHORS

Edward Fella; Rolf Fehlbaum; Maira & Tibor
Kalman; P. Scott & Laurie Haycock Makela;
Dorthe Meinhardt; North; Peter Rea; Michael Saup;
Tomato; Sven Voelker; Thomas Weiling.

ISBN 3-540-65589-1
Springer-Verlag
Berlin Heidelberg New York

Die Deutsche Bibliothek
CIP-Einheitsaufnahme

Beyond the Borders: Crossover in Creative Culture/
ed.: Rat für Formgebung/German Design Council.
Dorthe Meinhardt; Sven Voelker.
– Berlin; Heidelberg; New York; Barcelona;
Hongkong; London; Mailand; Paris; Singapur;
Tokio: Springer, 2000

PRINTING AND BINDING

Schneider Druck, Rothenburg o. d. Tauber
Schäffer, Grünstadt
SPIN 10709703
33/3142 – 2 – 543210

PAPER

Multi Art Silk 135 g/m² and 300 g/m²
from Papier Union

SCANS sponsored by
Headline, Bremen
Plantage 13, 28215 Bremen/Germany
headlinehb@aol.com

TRANSLATION

SATS Translation Services, Ehingen

ON

A COLD AND

CLEAR DAY YOU CAN SEE

THE HORIZON

AND BEYOND